LET THE INSIDE BE SWEET

The Interpretation of Music Event among the Kpelle of Liberia

RUTH M. STONE

INDIANA UNIVERSITY PRESS
Bloomington

Library of Congress Cataloging in Publication Data

Stone, Ruth M.
    Let the inside be sweet.

    Includes bibliography and index.
    1. Kpelle--Liberia--Music--History and criticism.
2. Folk music--Liberia--History and criticism. 3. Folksongs, Kpelle--Liberia--History and criticism.
4. Ethnomusicology. I. Title.
ML3760.S8   781.7666'2   81-48628
ISBN 0-253-33345-8   AACR2

To my mother and father

Contents

Illustrations

Kpelle Orthography

Tone Marks

kpólo	-high tone; when it appears on the stem of a word, it governs until another tone mark appears.
tòno	-low tone; when it appears on the stem of a word, it governs until another tone mark appears.
kâli konâ	-high-low compound tone; high tone on the first syllable followed by low tone on the next syllable, except when the tone mark appears on the last syllable of a word. In that case, the high-low occurs on that single syllable.
meni	-unmarked stem; denotes mid-tone throughout stem.

Consonants

gb	-g and b said together.
kp	-k and p said together.
ŋ	-as in sing.
ɣ	-y and g, sound somewhat like "ch" in German "ach."
ɓ	-like a b but with air going in rather than out when lips are closed.

Vowels

ɛ	-as in bet
ɔ	-as in caught, but shorter.

*The orthography is based on that developed by William Welmers and Otto Spehr for *Spoken Kpelle*. 1st rev. ed. Monrovia, Liberia, Lutheran Church in Liberia, 1956.

Music Transcription
Symbols

♩ sharp pitch but less than a semitone

♩ very sharp pitch but less than a semitone

♩ flat pitch but less than a semitone

♪ very flat pitch but less than a semitone

〰 glissando

𝄞₈ sounds an octave lower

Preface

Ba wule da meni taa-lolon lá,
If you hear a song from a town child,

ge ni daai tí su wule ká tí.
then it is the song of that town.

--Proverb

Personal experience influences the direction of
academic orientation and my situation bears this
out. The dissonance created by what I term "sound"
ethnomusicologists and "behavior" ethnomusicologists working in the same field of ethnomusicology
was especially evident in my own education for I
studied in two graduate programs that each emphasized a different extreme of this dichotomy. As a
result of working with some of the best minds who
advocate each aspect, I saw the strengths in each
approach. My search, as illustrated here, became
the quest for an approach that could bring these
two views into a tenacious unity.

In this spirit, I explore the "music event"
--first as a theoretical construct and then in a
particular field study application for a study
object that is analytically midway between the
analytical level of the dichotomous study objects
of the two groups. The event is grounded in the
details of performance but amenable to generalization at the broader systems level. Such a study
applauds the spirit of debate that has sparked the
research in the field on both sides and explores
possibilities for maintaining the vigor of each
approach even as it seeks an outlook that accom-
modates the other with an overarching framework.

The conclusions here argue that music events are
dynamically created by selecting and manipulating
facets of everyday life. Music both reflects and

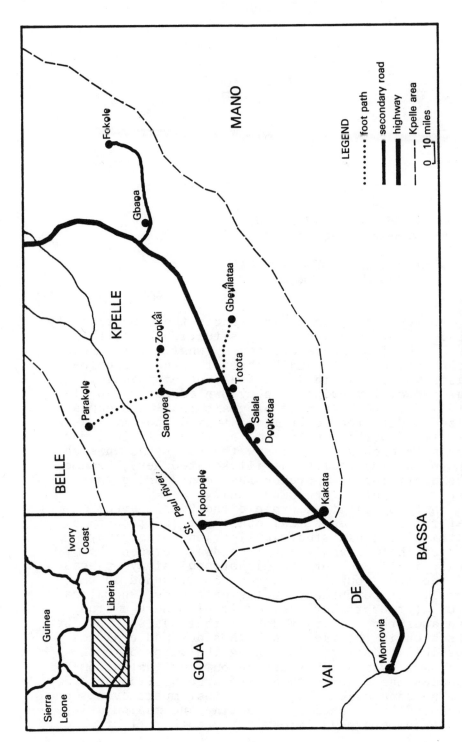

Map 1. Central Kpelle Area

restructures culture, and can only be understood as
we learn to interpret nuance, subtlety, and ambiguity in the processual creation of music performances. Such conclusions rely on a theoretical
orientation drawing from symbolic interactionism
and semiotic-cybernetic communication.

The Kpelle people live near the Guinea Coast of
West Africa; the southern boundary of their terri-
tory begins about forty miles inland in Liberia
and extends into Guinea (See Map 1). While they
call themselves *kpeℓe-ŋa*, they are referred to by
other variants of their name such as Pessi, Kpwesi,
Gberese, and in Guinea, Guerzé--all derivations of
names given them by other peoples (Welmers 1949:
209). Little research has centered on the regional
variations in language and culture, but as a whole,
the Kpelle in 1974 numbered approximately 250,000
in Liberia and 90,000 in Guinea (Liberia 1962;
1968; 1974; Picot 1958:273-86). James Gibbs has
written the most comprehensive ethnography of the
Kpelle (Gibbs 1960; 1965:197-240). In addition,
Richard Fulton has studied the Kpelle political
system, William Murphy the folklore, Beryl Bellman
ritual, and John Gay, Michael Cole and their associates have conducted psychological research (Fulton 1969; Murphy 1976; Bellman 1975; Gay and Cole
1967; Cole, et.al. 1971).

The Kpelle language, as classified by Joseph
Greenberg, is part of the Mande sub-family that
belongs to the larger Niger-Congo group of African
languages (Greenberg 1966:8). The evidence indicates that Kpelle speakers moved toward the coast
as part of the Mande migrations, beginning in the
fifteenth and continuing into the nineteenth century. As Warren d'Azevedo has pointed out, Liber-
ians have often been multi-lingual and have interacted extensively with other groups. During
the migrations and continuing into recent times,
shifting political alliances, trade, and the pan-
group Poro secret societies have all promoted
interaction among the various peoples (d'Azevedo
1962:512-38).

ETHNOGRAPHIC STUDIES

One of the earliest references to the Kpelle was
written by an English trader named Benjamin Harrison whose account of a journey across the Liberian

interior in the 1780s was published in April, 1808,
in the *Sierra Leone Gazette*. In his narrative he
mentioned areas through which he traveled, beginning among the Mende and proceeding eventually to
the Kpelle, which he called Beysee (Hair 1962:218-
26). Harrison's term, Beysee, was similar to the
name, Pessy, which two nineteenth-century writers,
Benjamin Anderson and Johann Büttikofer used in
reference to the Kpelle (Anderson 1870: map; Büttikofer 1890), but it was not until the twentieth
century that Maurice Delafosse first used the term
"kpêlé" in print (1900).

While little ethnographic literature concerning
Kpelle music exists, some historical value can be
gained by identifying those few sources which do
document early performance. An early reference
to Kpelle music appears in Sir Harry Johnston's
book, *Liberia*, in which he mentions *saɰwa* as a
Kpelle word for drum (Johnston 1906:1143). While
this word is rarely used in the central Kpelle
area to refer to drums, informants do recognize
it, but say it was not a Kpelle term originally.
Later sources mentioning Kpelle music focus on
names and descriptions of musical instruments or
activities, but to the present no extended study
of Kpelle music has examined structure, concepts,
behavior, function, or process.

The sources providing names of instruments and
musical activities are for the most part Kpelle
dictionaries. In Diedrich Westermann's Kpelle dictionary in *Die Kpelle-Sprache in Liberia*, general
definitions follow each of the terms. For example,
saɰwa féli is simply defined as a drum, but such
brief definition lacks details of interest to an
ethnomusicologist (Westermann 1924:208, 258).
William Welmer's mimeographed dictionary of Kpelle,
issued in 1948, includes a few more musical terms
and more detailed definitions. For example, he
defines *feli* as a "three-legged drum, usually held
between the knees and played with the hands" (1948:
8). J. Casthelain's 1952 dictionary based on the
Kpelle dialect spoken in Guinea, contains definitions which are more detailed than Westermann's,
providing, for example, six compounds employing
the word *woele* (song) (1952:279).

Discussions of musical instruments dominate the
literature, usually in the form of a listing of
the instruments and a description of their physical
features. Such description is the contribution of

Westermann's *Die Kpelle* to music ethnography, in
which are discussed transverse horns, chordophones,
flutes, and rattles (Westermann 1921:34). Cursory
descriptions of instruments also appear in the
report of the Harvard African Expedition (1926-27)
(Strong:64-66).

The third category of ethnographic literature
includes descriptions of musical activities, primarily from the French in Guinea; these were
written during the colonial period. Megrelis,
Holas, Lassort, and Germain, for example, published
numerous short descriptions that often mentioned
music events (Mengrelis 1946; 1948; 1951; 1952;
Holas 1953; Lassort 1947; 1951; Germain 1947; 1955).
For example, Mengrelis described the secret society,
Poro, and various music events associated with it
in four articles. In one account of a young women's
dance performance that entertained returning male
initiates, he concentrated on costumes, general
dance formations, the gourd rattle, and his interpretation of the emotional impact of the dance
(1951:44-46).

The ethnographic material on Kpelle music is
supported by the literature concerning the people
living in the area surrounding the Kpelle. Such
work is particularly relevant because of the long
history of interaction among the peoples of the
area.

The earliest written accounts of music in
Liberia are nineteenth-century observations of
travelers, missionaries, and scholars. D. W.
Whitehurst on a journey to Bopolu in 1835 described
a number of musical performances. He also provided
a detailed description of a drum and horn. The
drum he described as follows:

> The beating of the war drum is effected by the
> open hand, and requires great effort to accomplish
> it. The body of the drum resembles a mortar neatly
> fashioned, with places for the insertion of pieces
> of iron resembling a quiver, to which are attached
> rings of the same metal; the concussion of the drum
> head gives them a tremulous motion, which by bring-
> ing them into contact with the upright produces a
> jingling noise (1836:278).

Benjamin Anderson, on an 1868 journey, observed
a chief traveling from "Totaquella" to "Boporu"
accompanied by an entourage of praise-singing

musicians playing drums, horns, and a struck iron
idiophone (1870:31).

Johann Büttikofer, who began his travel in 1879,
provided early mention of Liberian music gleaned
during his explorations, describing various drums
and their uses without specifying the people among
whom he found them (1890:334-48). Paul Germann,
working primarily among the Gbande in the Bolahun
area, described musical instruments, and analyzed
what seems to be hocket technique in horn ensemble
performance, a practice widely documented in later
African literature (Germann 1933:62-66).

George Herzog was the first ethnomusicologist
to work in the Guinea Coast forest region inhabited
by the Kpelle and their neighbors, and his work
stands today as a brilliant contribution to the
field. His publications on signaling music and
language-music relationships among the Jabo (Glebo)
of southeastern Liberia are outstanding, and the
musical transcriptions are the first from this
area (1934; 1945; 1949).

The well-known works of George Harley and George
Schwab, among the Mano and Gio peoples respectively, provide descriptions of music and dance as
used in society, and Harley also analyzes the ritual uses of music (Harley 1950:3-5, 38-41; Schwab
1947:149-58). One of the most valuable features
of Schwab's work is the numerous photographs of
instruments, both alone and in the performance
context (1947; figs. 78-83, 93, 101); he also
makes some interesting observations about musical
timbre when he describes the various sounds made
by striking the head of the hourglass drum in different places (1947:151). Elsewhere he speaks of
a chordophone (triangular frame-zither) player as
being able to produce "... the yowling of a dog
or the shot of a gun" (1947:155).

André Schaeffner is another of the few ethnomusicologists who has worked in this area. His
work has centered on the area adjacent to the
northern Kpelle of Guinea, and his published work
offers extremely detailed descriptions of Kissi
musical instruments (1951).

During the last twenty years, much has been
written about the Liberian peoples of the Guinea
Coast area. Two Liberian scholars include Bai T.
Moore, Undersecretary of Information, Cultural
Affairs, and Tourism, who has delineated Liberian
song categories, and Agnes von Ballmoos who has

concentrated on the music of the nineteenth-century
repatriated African settler descendants (Moore
1970:117-37; von Ballmoos 1970:30-39). Many other
anthropologists and social scientists mention
musical activities, but the scholars whose work is
most relevant to the study of Kpelle music are
Warren d'Azevedo and Hugo Zemp, for their research
has centered on the study of the arts within the
cultural context.

In *The Artist Archetype in Gola Culture*, a mono-
graph which is focused on the study of behavior in
the arts with a concern for Gola aesthetic concepts, d'Azevedo included a brief analysis of dancers and musicians in Gola society in his work
(1966:41-44).

Hugo Zemp's book, *Musique Dan*, is the most extensive ethnomusicological study conducted within
this area to date (1971). Directed toward musical
behavior and the musical instruments involved in
that behavior, the work provides a good comparative study for Kpelle music. Although the Dan
live in neighboring Ivory Coast, they extend into
Liberia where they are known as Gio, and since Dan
and Kpelle are both Mande languages, the points
for comparison are extensive. Zemp's comments on
Dan ideas about music sound, classification of instruments, and performance practice are of special
interest; he is also one of the few scholars to
include in his musical texts the speeches that
occur between the songs (1971:204-205).

Visual and audio recordings of musical performances in Liberia date from the 1920s. In 1923,
H. Schomburgk made a silent film of dance associated with Sande (women's secret society) ritual
in northern Liberia: *Geheimbund-Riten der Frauen im
Liberia*, and Paul Germann filmed Gbande masked and
stilt dances in 1928 and 1929.[1] George Herzog
made 226 cylinder recordings in 1930 among the
Jabo, and in 1935 Robert Morey collected cylinder
recorded examples of Loma, Gbande, and Mandingo
music.[2] Although the Lebanese in Monrovia produced
limited edition commercial phonorecordings of
Liberian music earlier, the first American commercial recordings were issued by Packard L. Okie and
Arthur Alberts. In 1955 Okie, an Episcopalian
missionary, released *Folk Music of Liberia* con-
taining samples of music he collected from 1947 to
1954 in various areas of Liberia, including the
Kpelle.[4] Arthur Alberts, in his 1949 West African

trip, collected music of the Loma and Mano, as well
as the Fanti community on Marshall Island. He also
recorded songs of the settler descendants in Monrovia (1950; 1953; 1954).

Hans G. Himmelheber made six extended ethnographic research trips to Liberia and the Ivory
Coast between 1949 and 1965, during which he recorded Gio (Dan), Krahn, and Mano music. A phono-
recording accompanies his book *Die Dan* (1958). He
also produced numerous films for the Institut für
den Wissenschaftlichen Film that include visual and
sound recordings of music performances. In 1965-
66, Leo Sarkesian, working for Voice of America,
and Bai T. Moore undertook an extensive venture recording Liberian music, subsequently releasing a
sample album, *Music Time in Liberia* (ca. 1966-
1970).

Some recordings have been made for broadcast
over the Liberian radio stations. ELWA, a religious station, has made numerous recordings for
this purpose, as has the government supported station, ELBC. Music recordings made at the National
Cultural Center from many different Liberian peoples were aired in the series, *Legends and Songs of
Liberia*, from 1963-67.

It should be evident from the account of research in Liberia and among the Kpelle in particular that very little intensive and extended research has been conducted in the music and arts.
A rich area remains for exploration and this work
can reveal but a portion of the many facets that
may eventually be uncovered for us to comprehend.

This work is the result of many people contributing in diverse and often unique ways. The field
work and writing were conducted under a joint dissertation fellowship from Fulbright-Hays and the
Social Science Research Council; the African
Studies Program of Indiana University and its
Director, Patrick O'Meara, also provided assistance
and guidance during various phases of the project;
the Archives of Traditional Music at Indiana University furnished recording equipment and tape
stock through the courtesy of the Director, Frank
J. Gillis. The audiotape recordings and texts
referred to in the body of the dissertation are
deposited, along with accompanying translations, at
the Archives.

Many people in Liberia grasped the import of
research about Kpelle music and gave generously of

their knowledge and skill. I want to particularly
mention the two ensembles I studied intensively:
the Noni and Gbeyîlataa groups. I owe another
enormous debt to my research assistants, intermediaries and friends: Zau Gotoko and Yakpalo Don.
John McKay and Samuel Kennedy of the Kpelle Liter-
acy Center served as consultants on translation
problems; Bishop Roland Payne and his wife, Pris-
cilla, demonstrated keen interest that proved in-
valuable. Beverly Clinkingbeard patiently typed
several drafts of the manuscript. I want also to
mention the help of Bai T. Moore, Assistant Minis-
ter of Information, Cultural Affairs, and Tourism;
Agnes von Ballmoos, Assistant Professor of Music
at the University; Dr. Marie Antoinette Brown Sher-
man, President of the University of Liberia, Ginny
and Gerry Currens, Ted and Jane Leidenfrost, Dionne
and Bill Marquardt, Gloria Swanson, Geoffrey Thompson, and Jay Clinkingbeard.

My teachers, colleagues, and students have at
various times read and patiently critiqued parts
of this manuscript. Among these I wish to per-
sonally thank Warren L. d'Azevedo, who is a fellow
researcher in Liberia; Richard M. Dorson, who encouraged innovation in research and precision in
writing expression; the late Alan P. Merriam who
was both teacher and colleague and consistently
challenged those in search of knowledge; Roy Sieber,
who offered insight and encouragement; Ronald R.
Smith for gracious comment and a collegial relationship; Pamela Feldman and Bruce Conforth who
worked as enthusiastic research assistants.

My family, including my parents and parents-in-
law have, in special ways, encouraged the comple-
tion of this work. Angela Keema, my daughter who
was born in the midst of this project, merits
thanks for the patience and good humor she has
shown in sharing my attention with this work.
Finally, my husband, Verlon L. Stone, has participated more intimately than anyone else in this
production, providing research assistance in recording, photography, and graphics as well as per-
ceptive suggestions. He deserves my lasting appreciation.

I would like to gratefully acknowledge permission
from the publishers to reprint portions of the following articles: "Let the Inside Be Sweet: Strategies for Communication in Kpelle Music Events," in

Folklore on Two Continents: Essays in Honor of Linda Dégh, ed. Nikolai Burlakoff and Carl Lindahl (Bloomington: Trickster Press, 1980), pp. 233-41.

   "Toward a Kpelle Conceptualization of Music Performance," *Journal of American Folklore* 94:188-206; "Event, Feedback and Analysis: Research Media in the Study of Music Events," *Ethnomusicology* 25:215-25.

                                                    R.M.S.

Bloomington, Indiana
February 15, 1982

LET THE INSIDE BE SWEET

BE SWEET

The Interpretation of Music Event among the Kpelle of Liberia

1
Music as Event

Zu é née.
Let the inside be sweet.

                              --Comment by audience member at
                                  beginning of event

Music event as a study object possesses conceptual validity from the Kpelle perspective. For the
Kpelle music sound is conceived as part of an integrally related cluster of dance, speech, and
kinesic-proxemic behavior referred to as *pêle* and
occurring in particular time-space dimensions. We
shall argue, by extension, that the event also has
methodological validity for ethnomusicology in
general.
    The Kpelle term *pêle* glosses certain music
events as well as a broader spectrum of human behavior including games.[1] Music may be *pêle*, but
not all music is *pêle*, nor, as in the case of
games, is all *pêle*, music. Several events an
ethnomusicologist might label music performance
are not considered part of the category *pêle*.
These omissions from *pêle* extend to all types of
work songs, *tîi-ke-wule*, such as those played for
bush clearing, planting, and harvest, including
the performance of funeral dirges, *zama-pilîi*--
literally "throw" *zama*. *Zere-kê*, praise singing,
is not considered *pêle* when a single individual
performs in a situation where group interaction is
insignificant, such as the lack of a responding
chorus. A musician playing a solo instrument is
not engaged in *pêle*. *Pêle* is predicated on group
interaction of a particular quality involving multiple media.
    The music event may assume quite different forms
when delineated by different cultures. Some peo-

1

ple, like the Kpelle, incorporate more than music,
for Kpelle music events envelop units of song as
well as other types of interaction such as dance
and speeches given during pauses in the music by
the audience or performers as evaluation of the
performance. The event consists of the participants' dynamic processes of evaluation and action,
creating the interaction from which the event's
meaning is derived.

As a unit of study, the Kpelle music event is a
bounded sphere of interaction. That is, it is set
off and made distinct from the world of everyday
life by the participants. Most ethnomusicologists
assume that music performance is distinct from
other activities in a culture. Yet the exact ways
in which events are bounded to make them distinct
are largely unexplored in the field. Little discussion exists in the literature of how different
peoples set off music performance from everyday
life or other areas of reality.

In this study, music event, with the Kpelle
example offering primary data, is considered as one
of the "privileged operational zones of a culture,"
a term James Boon uses to describe contexts, distinct from everyday life, in which "cultural operations" are being carried out. In these contexts
the participants are selecting and interrelating
sets of elements from various cognitive orders of
phenomena in complex ways (1973:10).

The Kpelle consider events to be distinct from
everyday life. They distinguish between the "inside" of the performance and the "outside" of the
performance. A performer says, "Kwa loi belei su"
(We are entering the inside of the performance).
Actions are categorized as taking place inside or
outside the sphere of *pêle*.

These privileged operational zones are compar-
able to Alfred Schutz's notion of "finite spheres,"
those provinces of meaning distinct from everyday
life and within which the experiences are made
"meaning compatible" (1973:119). As a Kpelle triangular frame-zither *(konîn)* player plucks a string
he may be connecting a particular social order
position--that of chief--within a finite sphere of
musical meaning. Meanings created here, by performers and audience alike, unite sound orders as
well as behavior orders, for here they are related
by the participants to each other and to many other

aspects of culture as well through interaction.

As connections are made between cognitive orders --and a myriad are made during a single moment of performance--the elements become interrelated, though the nature of that relationship is not always the same. In some instances, the conjunction may exhibit a crystallized form typical of a symbol, but in others it may not be bound at any level. Boon suggests the term "cultural operators," incorporating bounded symbols as well as less bounded forms. He defines cultural operators as the "succinct and orderly conjunction of elements from what appear to the analyzer, to the actors, or both, as diverse orders" (1973:10). The skill of a 'Kpelle performer lies in bringing into unity elements that in another context might appear to have no evident relationship. When the conjunction of elements does not appear bound, the research focus is on the connection between orders rather than upon the form of the higher level object. Cultural operators serve to create connection between the performance event and other aspects of culture, connecting elements that in everyday life may appear dissimilar and unrelated.

Music, in the form of *wule* (song) and *mãla* (dance), offers the possibility for dense communication of ideas and feelings within the context of *pêle*. That is, within a relatively short period of interaction, many, many ideas can be presented which have the quality of *sâu*.

Sâu is a quality of experience that is characteristically multi-faceted, multi-interpretable, subtle, indirect, aesthetically pleasing, and created in the conjunction of elements from diverse orders. *Sâu* reveals experience through exposure of facets and in exposure of these facets, emphasis is not on the disparity of parts but rather on the new creation, the new unity. Richard Brown's definition of metaphor is similar to the concept of *sâu* when he comments that metaphor "conveys an impact and connotative richness not achievable by conventional description." Iconic metaphor in particular, he says, "allows us to *apprehend* what the particular is in its uniqueness" (1977:78, 85-86). The employment of *sâu* might also be termed "thick performance," extending Clifford Geertz's term "thick description" (1973:6-7). The Kpelle consider *sâu* to be the essence of *pêle*, but *sâu* is

applicable to the connections of diverse orders apparent in a dance pattern, a verbal proverb, a song
phrase, or even a piece of tie-dyed cloth.

Sân makes performance multi-interpretable; no
single meaning is conceived as being the only or
proper one. In fact, Kpelle people delight in de-
bating the many possible interpretations. Sân
makes performance subtle and indirect; ambiguity
about possible implications of connections is valued. Sân in performance implies that a small,
knowledgeable in-group will understand the communication and often express this delight in extensive
verbalization about its qualities.

The Kpelle comment on the nature of sân with
statements such as the following:

Sân no 6e pa a wulei.
Only sân brought about song.

Wule tooo 6a sân tee tee, nyan zu-kûlai tamaai.
Singing involves many, many sân and the meanings are
    many.

Kwa kpele-woo tono síye, ku bène péne é seri lóolu.
We take one Kpelle word (in performance), we turn it,
    turn it, as many as five times.

PARTICIPANTS

While the study object is the event, the locus
of the interest in this event is the participants'
interaction. In focusing on the interaction with
all its idiosyncrasies and incongruities, we are
looking at musical meaning as "world producing"
rather than as simply a product of the nature of
things (Berger and Luckmann 1966:89). Such recognition is profoundly important for it acknowledges
the centrality of meaning created in interaction.

The participants in music events include both
the individuals producing music and the people experiencing the music performance as listeners or
audience, and the auditors' meanings and interpretations are just as significant as those of the
performers. As Blacking has noted, "creative,
critical listening is a sign of musical competence
no less than is musical performance (1971b:30).

In many cultures, the distinction between performer and audience is not a clear nor static di-

chotomy. Therefore, audience, performer, and participant are considered "sensitizing" concepts,
pending further research clarifying the definitions and distinctions for particular situations
in particular cultures. In this study, participants include anyone designated as sharing in the
event's interactions. This may be an instrumen-
talist, a dancer, a soloist, a chorus member, a
performance chief, a master of ceremonies, or an
audience member, for example.

PÊLE

To better understand what the performance of
pêle implies, a synopsis of the phases of one *pêle*
which we attended follows:

Day 1--The performance chief from a neighboring town sends
a message that a death feast will be held in three days.
He requests that the Gbeyilataa group come to perform.
The messenger presents a token gift as he makes the request. The Gbeyilataa performance chief consults with the
performers who agree to the engagement. The performance
chief informs the town chief of the upcoming engagement.

Day 3--Afternoon--The drummers gather to tune the drums by
unlacing and restringing them. The performers gradually
assemble and begin walking together to the neighboring town.

Dusk--As the Gbeyîlataa group approaches the town, they
put their instruments in place, situating their wooden
props for the *koli-gôu-sôu* performance above their heads.
As they approach the path's intersection with the village,
the performers start playing, processing counter-clockwise around the outer perimeter of the village. The
master of ceremonies leads the procession of singers,
dancers, instrumentalists and chorus members. Children
and townspeople join the procession as it moves. As the
performers complete their round, they move to the house
of their patron. The performance chief speaks to the
patron and officially announces the group's arrival with
a token. The patron responds with a token. He then presents the performance chief to the local political leaders. The group disbands and people mingle as the crowd
gathers. The performance chief continues negotiation
with the patron, periodically returning to consult with
the group about terms of the arrangements.

Dark--The group shares a bottle of gin given by the
patron. They begin playing and the group dances.
The crowd moves in a "wheel," following one another
and moving counterclockwise. The group dance ends
as the master of ceremonies calls for a pause. An
audience member makes a speech in praise of the performers. The performers pause to share more gin.

The master of ceremonies clears the area, opening
space for the solo dancers who perform next. A
series of men and women come into the dance area one
at a time. One particularly fine dancer receives
numerous tokens from various audience members.

The patron asks the master of ceremonies to call
for another pause in the event. During the pause,
the patron makes a speech explaining the occasion
and encouraging the musicians to play better. He
presents the group with another bottle of gin.

The performers once more move in procession
from one house to another, playing for certain
households. After stopping at five houses, the
performers return to the central arena. Again the
master of ceremonies arranges the crowd for a solo
dance performance. After about two hours of playing, the group pauses to eat a meal provided by
the patron. Then the group resumes playing for
the night. Alternate performers give the principal performers a chance to rest at various times.

Day 4--Daybreak--The musicians are given more
liquor. They begin to perform with renewed vigor
as the crowd increases. The sacrifices for the
death feast are made. The animals killed are
then cooked for the feast.

Midmorning--Food is presented to the musicians
and family members and the music stops as everyone
eats. The performance then resumes for a short
time. The patron calls for a pause, thanks the
performers, and gives them a leave-taking token.
The performers depart for their home playing as
they leave the village.

PERFORMANCE PROCESS

Interaction and communication within music events
have scarcely been studied as process. To do so
involves a concern for change as well as the trans-

mission, reception, and feedback processes. The
implications for incorporating process into ethnomusicological studies at the level of event are
profound; rather than looking at a series of objects frozen in time and space,

> every facet of apprehension is itself a consti-
> tuted unity of duration....The possibility exists
> in reflection of looking to the constituted lived
> experience and the constituting phases and even
> becoming aware of the differences that exist (Husserl
> 1964:163).

Ethnomusicologists can explicitly examine responses
to music performance as well as the performance
itself. They must be then concerned with the ebb
and flow that is part of building a music event,
considering process in music events to entail
analysis of the multiple dimensions of time as
participants experience them.

ASSUMPTIONS ABOUT EVENTS

The assumptions underlying any study constitute
the conceptual framework from which the ethnomusicologist approaches the task. We include,
therefore, some of the assumptions implicit in the
present attitude of study toward the music event.

Music is communication. The performer plans and
creates music performance which is audited and experienced by other performers and event participants. The performers synchronize their actions,
fitting their performances with those of other
participants. The auditors interpret the performance according to each of their relevances and
respond to the performers. This, in its simplest
form, is music communication.
Music communication is multi-channeled. Music
communication utilizes the audio-acoustic channel,
as well as other channels such as the kinesthetic-
visual and tactile. While most ethnomusicologists
concentrate primarily on the audio-acoustic, preliminary evidence indicates that in many cultures
other channels are intimately linked to the audio-
acoustic. Dance among the Kpelle, for example, is
nearly inseparable from sound in music performance.

Multiple channels can operate at differential
levels at any one time and may use different
codes (Birdwhistell 1970:70).

*Music communication is a dynamic, ongoing sym-
bolic process in which participants--performer and
audience--interpret the meaning of symbolic behavior.*

*Meaning in music is created by participants in
the course of social interaction.* Meaning is a
social product formed and maintained as the participant interprets the activities of people with
whom he interacts.

> Social interaction [read musical interaction] is a
> process that *forms* human conduct instead of being
> merely a means or a setting for the expression or
> the release of human conduct (Blumer 1969:2, 8).

Meaning is not something inherent in an object,
event, symbol, or any other phenomenon.

*Meaning in music events is created with refer-
ence to the immediate event situation, past personal and cultural experience, and current relevances in conjunction with anticipated response.*
As the participant in a music event creates meaning, he does so by referring to knowledge he has
about the present performance, his stock of knowledge about music in general, as well as other
aspects of culture that bear on the interaction of
the present moment. Past experience, for example,
may also be important in shaping performance behavior.

*The construction of meaning in music events in-
volves an interpretive process whereby participants
relate the potential information in a music event
to a dynamic, updatable cognitive map and their own
purposeful state.* Communication theory, specifically that connected with the semiotic-cybernetic
model, labels the interpretive process. The individual cognitive map, existing in a purposeful
state, is transformed as a result of the interpretation of environmental stimuli, this transfor-
mation resulting in specific goal-directed behavior
(Nauta 1972:65).

*Much music communication is routine and the
meanings are typified or taken-for-granted.* The
interpretive process operates at an out-of-awareness level when meanings are taken-for-granted.

A musical communicative situation that ceases to be routine and thus requires active interpretation is said to become problematic. In such an instance, the interpretive process operates within the individual's awareness or consciousness.

Subjective meaning is truth for the event participants. The participants, be they performer or auditor, derive their meaning from their relevances and assessment of the situation (Hansen 1974). The assessment of any individual is not necessarily shared with other event participants since their experiences and interpretations of experiences are not identical.

The social relationship among event participants is based upon the simultaneous experiencing of the performance in multiple dimensions of time. Participants live through multi-dimensional time as they orient themselves to the actions of one another. The exact description of the time dimensions awaits more ethnomusicological data, but Alfred Schutz has identified at least one possibility. He speaks of the distinction between "inner" and "outer" time, while Blacking, for example, distinguishes "virtual" or "actual" time (1973:27).[2] Outer time is homogeneous and measurable by such devices as clocks and metronomes. Inner time exists for participants when they are "participating in an interplay of recollections, retentions, protentions, and anticipations which interrelate the successive elements" (Schutz 1964:170). Two performances measured as lasting the same length of time in outer time could seem very different in length to the participants experiencing the elements in an inner time dimension.

Inner time, which Bergson calls *durée*, occurs within the stream of consciousness and does not contain homogeneous units of measure (Schutz 1964:170). The rhythm of inner time can be conceived as "flying stretches and resting places of the stream of consciousness" according to William James (1890, 1:243). As music is created, it is constituted step-by-step or polythetically in inner time (Schutz and Luckmann 1973:53).

The ethnomusicologist makes inferences about music event interaction by engaging in interactional behavior. As ethnomusicologists seek to understand musical interaction, they also engage in a social process, whether observing an event or

conducting an interview. They construct an explanation of the event by making the kinds of inferences Schutz refers to as "second-order" constructs. These are necessarily different from the
participants' "first-order" constructs (Schutz and
Luckmann 1973:62).

2

Toward an Event Perspective

> To commit ourselves to a paradigm is thus to sub-
> mit to a double uncertainty. We must rely on the
> formalism of our theory or art work in order to
> apprehend its contents, yet this formalism is always
> subject to reformulation in light of our experience
> with these contents. This paradox is inevitable for
> the questioning mind.
>   --Richard H. Brown (1977b:43)

The rationale for choosing "event" as a focal
study object is rooted in the historical under-
pinnings of ethnomusicological thought and research. A schism in ethnomusicology has, particularly in the United States, separated scholars
who study music sound from scholars who study
music behavior. Such a schism, perhaps less
sharply visible in the present, has derived, in
part, from anthropological and musicological
approaches applied to the study of music. The
result has been that the study object has not
been the same for all ethnomusicologists. Some
scholars have studied "music sound," other scholars have studied "music behavior," and those who
have attempted to encompass both sound and behavior in a single project have often approached
each aspect in fundamentally different ways, and
at differing analytical levels. Quite predict-
ably the final result has been an unwieldy bond
of the sound and behavior elements, lacking integrated parts.[1]

The situation as just outlined has not, in
fact, been as crystal clear and simple in detail.
The musicology/anthropology split has been also
characterized as a kind of humanities/social
science split (Merriam 1964:17-31). Recent devel-

opments in the field, however, complicate such a
neat division. First, a small but ambitious group
of ethnomusicologists, including Jean-Jacques
Nattiez as its most prolific advocate, has turned
to semiotics to formalize music sound analysis
(1977:121-42). Such formalism derives from the
sciences in certain respects and crosses the
science/humanities boundary. Furthermore, ethnomusicologists concerned with sound measurement use
such devices as the melograph in ways clearly deriving from the natural and social sciences. These
sound-ethnomusicologists have deviated from the
humanities perspective, adopting techniques, and by
extension, some of the underlying assumptions, of
the sciences.[2]

On the other side, behavior-ethnomusicologists
have also bridged the gap. In some recent studies,
those scholars in anthropology drawing on symbolic
interactionism and phenomenological sociology are
clearly moving toward humanistically oriented paradigms. They focus on smaller units of behavior
than culture systems and are consequently more
oriented toward micro-analysis of human interaction
than scholars looking at culture more broadly.
They also consider the study of emotion and feelings, those aspects of behavior often excluded from
scientific studies.

As a consequence, one cannot apply the social
science/humanities labels to the behavior- and
sound-ethnomusicologists without some modifications.
Recent trends indicate that the former are drawing
on humanistic philosophies and the latter are
drawing on the sciences for method and technique.
Furthermore, both have drawn upon the disciplines
of folklore and sociology, among others, as these
disciplines have turned to studies of small groups
analogous to those of micro-analytical studies of
humanistic philosophies. Furthermore, folklore has
long been oriented to studying verbal texts, the
products of behavior.

Ethnomusicologists of both viewpoint extremes
continually claim that ethnomusicology is an interdisciplinary field (Nettl 1964:15-16). I maintain,
however, that in practice these several disciplines
have never been well integrated into the work of
ethnomusicology (Merriam 1964:15). In fact, at
times when ethnomusicologists have lacked their own
clear direction, they have applied theories and

methodologies developed for other study objects and communicative systems to their data. In certain cases, they have applied these strategies without clearly understanding their utility or the underlying assumptions. This problem is exemplified in the adoption of linguistic models for studying music (Feld 1974:197-217). In short, asserting that ethnomusicology is interdisciplinary has provided an excuse and escape from searching for more powerful and elegant ways of studying music creation in human communities and has left most scholars without a "mission" to develop a paradigm for ethnomusicology.

To develop systematic procedures in ethnomusicology does not deny that competing models and paradigms exist. But failing to make the attempt implies that ethnomusicology is a field so like some other field that it needs no special procedure based on an underlying theoretical orientation.

ASSUMPTIONS

In seeking possible directions for uniting sound and behavior we must first examine and evaluate some of the implicit assumptions underlying the two fundamental approaches that have developed in the United States since the founding of the Society for Ethnomusicology. The assumptions reveal perspectives that must be taken into account in developing approaches to ethnomusicology, and bring into awareness those underlying principles basic to the pursuit of research.

Study Object

We can begin by considering the principles undergirding the choice and delimitation of study object. The sound-ethnomusicologist has made the following implicit assumption:

1.1 *The primary study object is music sound.* Though human behavior occurs in conjunction with the production of music sound, it is the goal of the sound-oriented researcher to consider sound as the central study object. Behavior and context, while acknowledged, are always peripheral and subsidiary to sound, the auditory phenomena. In con-

trast, the behavior-ethnomusicologist has assumed
the following:

   1.2 *The primary study object is music behavior
that produces music sound.* Here the focal interest of study is the social action that creates a
sound product; the behavior-ethnomusicologist considers this action as antecedent to the sound itself.   Therefore, one set of scholars studies certain phenomena and the other set studies different
phenomena that are considered to precede and underlie the first phenomena.

   Aside from the choice of study object, the following is the case for the sound-ethnomusicologist:

   2.1 *Music sound is an independent system, with
structure inherent in the system.* Yet from the
perspective of the behavior-ethnomusicologist, a
different assumption is implicit:

   2.2 *Music is a system of behavior integrally
related to other systems within the culture.* The
work in this area has derived largely from the
structural-functionalist framework that considers
culture as an organic whole of interrelated parts.
David Ames' study comparing musician roles in Igbo
and Hausa societies in Nigeria exemplifies this
assumption (1973:250-73).

   The first difficulty in seeking a unitary approach to ethnomusicology arises because the study
object is fundamentally different in the two approaches. Behavior-oriented researchers look at
behavior, and sound-oriented researchers look at
sound. Furthermore, behavior as an object is
situated within a larger system of behavior. In
contradistinction, sound is constituted as an object that is a system unto itself.

Context

   Ethnomusicological assumptions concerning context parallel those involving study object. For
the sound-ethnomusicologist the following assumption can be stated:

   3.1 *Context is adjacent rather than integral
to sound.* While the ethnomusicologist concentrating on sound acknowledges contest as legiti-
mate in research, this acknowledgment has brought
a very careful compartmentalization. This separation underlies Charles Seeger's statement, "Clearly we must study music both in itself and in cul-

ture...." (McAllester and McCollester 1959:101).
It is also particularly evident in the definition
of ethnomusicology provided by Mantle Hood; in the
Harvard Dictionary of Music he says,

> Ethnomusicology is an approach to the study of *any*
> music, not only in terms of itself but also in
> relation to its cultural context (1969:298).

That is, though recognizing context, one can still
separate it from the fundamental concern of a
sound-ethnomusicologist. The careful division of
ethnomusicological studies into one section on
music sound and another on music ethnography accom-
plishes this. Context, for the sound-ethnomusicologist, often means context as constituted in the
related arts. For example, Mantle Hood in giving
examples of cultural context for the Japanese *koto*
includes different types of *koto*, distinctive style
periods of literature for the instrument, related
instruments, the history of Japanese arts, and the
other art forms (1971:31-32). This use of context
concentrates on the "things" adjacent to the music
sounds being considered.
    On the other hand, the behavior-ethnomusicologist
assumes the following:
    3.2 *Context is integral to the study of music
behavior*. Because this ethnomusicologist often
works from a structural-functionalist perspective,
context is of interest for relating music behavior
to other parts of the culture system. Therefore,
while context is important for the behavior-ethnomusicologist, it is secondary for the sound-ethnomusicologist. Context is integral to a researcher
whose paradigm stresses interrelatedness. But
context is adjacent and separate for the researcher
who draws on a tradition emphasizing compartmentalization.

Analytic Level

    The term "analytic level" distinguishes varying
degrees of research specificity: the study of "song"
is much more specific than the consideration of
"musical repertoire." It is crucial that analytic
level be distinguished when comparing approaches.
In the work of the sound-ethnomusicologist the following assumption concerning analytic level is implicit:

4.1 *Music sound is studied at the analytic level of song*. Researchers transcribe and analyze entities of music sound segmented into research units called "songs." This focus is particularly evident in tape recordings that select song segments from the total event. Further, music transcriptions are presented as units of sound enveloped as songs. Work at this analytic level was typical even of the work of the predecessors to ethnomusicology. Guido Adler in 1885 referred to comparative musicology as

*die vergleichende Musikwissenschaft, die sich zur
Aufgabe macht, die Tonproducte, insbesondere die
Volksgesänge verschiedner Völker, Länder, und
Territorien behufs ethnographischer Zwecke zu
vergleichen und nach der Verschiedenheit ihrer
Beschaffenheit zu gruppiren und sondern.*

comparative musicology which has as its task the
comparison of the sound products, especially the
folksongs, of the various peoples, countries, and
territories for ethnographical purposes, and the
classification of them according to their various
natures (Adler 1885:14).

In the work of the behavior-ethnomusicologist, the following assumption concerning analytic level is implicit:

4.2 *Music behavior is studied at the analytic level of system*. Music is studied as it exhibits organization, rules, and norms and interlocks with social structure, political structure and other parts of culture. The behavior-ethnomusicologist seeks to explain the rules whereby a music system exists for a particular people and how this entity fits with the larger system of culture.

As a result of these two disparate analytic levels, the study object is not only quite different, but the degree of specificity with which the study object is considered is dissimilar. The sound-ethnomusicologist works at the micro-level, the behavior-ethnomusicologist at the macro-level (Merriam 1969:222; 1975:64). Even when both aspects of music are considered in the same study, they are examined at very different levels. If a unitary approach is to be developed, resolving the disparity of analytic levels becomes crucial. The phenomenon and its study are quite different if

one is considering songs rather than songs and their
associated behavior and how it all fits together
in the larger cultural context. Crucial details to
one study become insignificant bits of data in the
other when each is conceived at a different analytic level.

This disparity in determining the suitable study
object also implies a difference in definition of
the context. The sound-ethnomusicologist assumes
the following in regard to context:

5.1 *Context is studied at a specific level
corresponding to the specific level of sound
studied.* For the sound-ethnomusicologist, context
is interpreted to mean either the adjacent sound
within a music system or the adjacent art forms.
The behavior-ethnomusicologist, however, assumes
the following:

5.2 *Context is studied at a general level corresponding to the general approach to a music system.* For the behavior-ethnomusicologist context is
that area of human behavior comprising systems that
are related to the music system. In regard to
analytic level, we must resolve the problem of a
tradition in ethnomusicology that considers sound
and behavior at two very different levels. This
difference can be compared roughly to the difference between looking at an object with the naked
eye or examining it under a microscope.

The designation of levels seems to be multiply-
ing in recent ethnomusicological studies. John
Blacking speaks of "surface" versus "deep" levels
in drawing on structuralist terminology (Blacking
1971a:91-108). Various scholars refer to "etic"
versus "emic" levels, linguistic terms that have
entered folkloric and anthropological vocabulary
(Boilès and Nattiez 1977:45). Nattiez points out
the "poietic," "neutral," and "esthesic" dimensions
of music in reference to semiotic perspectives
(1977:134-36). These terms all represent attempts
to formalize the analysis of music. But each must
be defined according to its use in ethnomusicology,
with reference both to the original and present
assumptions implicit in the usage in a particular
discipline.

Research Framework

In respect to research framework, the following assumption is implicit in the work of the sound-ethnomusicologist:

6.1 *Theory, method, and techniques are implicit and sometimes eclectic.* An ethnomusicologist of this perspective takes his *modus operandi* for granted. He devotes little space to explaining the theoretical orientation, for superstructure is of secondary importance to the final description and analysis. The work of the semiotic-ethnomusicologist is a notable exception, for such a researcher usually explains the theory, methodology, and techniques involved in a particular study (Nattiez 1977:121-42).[3]

The behavior-ethnomusicologist makes quite the opposite assumption from that of the sound-ethno-musicologist.

6.2 *Theory, method, and techniques are usually explicitly stated.* The behavior-ethnomusicologist does explicate the procedures and underlying frame-work of a study; this concern with research mechanics reflects his social scientific training. These explicit and implicit frameworks yield further assumptions concerning research procedures. For the sound-ethnomusicologist, one can assume the following:

7.1 *Songs are analyzed primarily as products.* The ethnomusicologist is concerned with the examination of sound "things" or "objects." He looks at static sound structures, dissects them, and examines the components such as scale, rhythm, and melodic intervals. This approach is due, in part, to the transcription of sound into Western musical notation, a system which designates music as a series or conglomerate of points in two-dimensional space rather than as a flow of audio phenomena (Nettl 1964:98-130).

On the other hand, the behavior-ethnomusicologist operates under the following assumption:

7.2 *Behavior is analyzed primarily as a product resulting from rules and norms.* Here behavior becomes the object to be analyzed in the same way that sound was the sound-ethnomusicologist's object of analysis. For the behavior-ethnomusicologist, music behavior results from the concepts or ideas that people have about what constitutes appropriate

musical activity. One of the most thorough discussions of the study of music behavior from this
perspective is Alan P. Merriam's work, *The Anthropology of Music* (1964).

In further considering the research framework,
we can also explore the assumptions underlying the
goal of research. For the sound-ethnomusicologist
it can be summarized as follows:

8.1 *Description and analysis are primary; generalization and explanation are seldom attempted
or realized.* From this point of view, theory as
an explanation of data is an ideal attainable only
after a great deal of data is assembled. The
sound-ethnomusicologist often considers it unwise
to attempt generalization, preferring to continue
gathering data. As Charles Seeger has said,

> The natural and social sciences have advanced from
> positions of main reliance upon analytical tech-
> niques to bold syntheses of universal proportions,
> while in musicology, even mention of synthesis is
> not quite respectable (1968:33).

In contrast, the behavior-ethnomusicologist
operates under the following assumption:

8.2 *The goal of research is to explain behavior
and to make generalization possible.* This scholar
attempts to arrive at broad conclusions, which he
feels are necessary if research is to have application beyond a specific study. In making such generalizations, he acknowledges that revision of
these conclusions is both normal and to be expected
when data becomes available.

Some inherent assumptions are common to both
sound- and behavior-ethnomusicologists. In terms
of study object, the following assumption obtains:

9.0 *The study object is considered to be a
product.* Researchers of both extremes consider
products as the main focus of study, contrasting
with "process" which might also be studied. The
concern with product means that discrete entities
are the items of data manipulated so that the ebb
and flow of performance communication is not considered.

Researchers of both extremes have also assumed
the following:

10.0 *The ethnomusicologist is an objective observer.* That is, the ethnomusicologist is able to
supersede his personal and cultural biases and

regard the music from a relatively neutral position.[4]

In summary, although ethnomusicologists have
generally studied product and considered the ethnomusicologist to be an objective observer, the differences remain. A fundamental division in the
field results from dissimilar structures undergirding and ever-influencing study. Furthermore,
since some scholars may not explicate their underlying framework, discerning points of disagreement
becomes even more difficult. And when the frameworks include differing research goals, the division between the two approaches becomes profound.

In the last twenty years of ethnomusicology's
history, these diverse approaches have served
useful purposes, for each has helped to elucidate
particular data that the other has not. Yet if
ethnomusicology is to unify the study of music
sound and behavior, we must continually seek to
clarify confusions, evaluating theories, and
searching for ways of elucidating that which we
deem to be significant.

MUSIC AS EVENT

The base for conceptualizing "music as event"
draws on research in sociology, anthropology,
linguistics, and folklore, as well as on work of
ethnomusicologists who have reflected this approach
in some way (Merriam 1975:62; Besmer 1974).

George Herzog, an early American ethnomusicologist, sought a real conjunction of sound and behavior. His training in music with Erich M. von
Hornbostel, anthropology with Franz Boas, and
linguistics with Edward Sapir provided an interdisciplinary preparation that few ethnomusicologists then or since have possessed. Some of his
ideas emerged in several articles on Jabo music
of Liberia where he presented Jabo concepts concerning the organization of music (Herzog 1934:452-
66, 1945:217-38, 1949:196-97).

David McAllester, one of Herzog's students, also
moved in this direction. In *Enemy Way Music*,
McAllester demonstrated that cultural values were
connected and similar to values concerning music
performance (1954). Somewhat later, Alan P. Merriam
set forth ways in which anthropology could assist in

the study of music sound. *The Anthropology of Music*
drew attention to the study of the behavioral context of music with such force that few ethnomusicological studies are written now without at least
a token bow to behavior and context (1964).

Alan Lomax, John Blacking, and Charles Boilès
each drew specific conclusions in quite different
ways regarding the nature of the sound-behavior
link. Lomax considered song style, broadly conceived, to "portray some level of human adapta-
tion, some social style" (1968:8). John Blacking,
in *Venda Children's Songs*, inferred that the
pitches of many children's songs were transposed
variations of the most important item of Venda
music, the Venda national dance, and has continued
in subsequent work to explore other dimensions of
the connection (1967:191-98). Charles Boilès explored the sound-behavior connection on a more
specific level than Blacking or Lomax and concluded
that pitch order, for example, communicated the
presence of specific deities or the movements of
deities in Tepehua ritual ceremonies (1967:267-92).

Some ethnomusicologists have explored the
boundaries of the music domain and this research
offers important insights and considerations for
definition of event. The dissertations of Charles
R. Adams (1974), Nahoma Sachs (1975), and Carol
Robertson-DeCarbo (1975) are good examples of different approaches. George List's consideration of
music sound/speech relationships also poses questions
about boundaries from the analytical perspective
(List 1963:1-16). Hugo Zemp's recent attempts to
make explicit 'Are'Are concepts of music theory are
also important in this regard (1979:5-48).
Such is the case as well with Adrienne L. Kaeppler's earlier work in regard to dance concepts
(1972:173-217). These studies point out how carefully we need to question the very definition and
bounding of event.

"Event" has been used by some scholars synony-
mously with "performance." Event can be defined
as, "the actual fact of anything happening; the
occurrence of," though the Oxford English Dictionary points out that "in modern usage event is
usually restricted to occurrences of some importance" (1971:907). Performance is defined as "the
accomplishment, execution, carrying out, working
out of anything ordered or undertaken" (1971:2132).

In ethnomusicology, some scholars have identified "music event" and made initial attempts to
study it. Norma McLeod in 1966 used the term "musical occasion" as a term similar in concept and
scope. Marcia Herndon elaborated the concept when
she said,

> The musical occasion, then, may be regarded as an
> encapsulated expression of the shared cognitive
> forms and values of a society, which includes not
> only the music itself but also the totality of
> associated behavior and underlying concepts. It is
> usually a named event, with a beginning and an end,
> varying degrees of organization of activity, aud-
> ience performances, and location (1971:340).

This definition presented an important attempt
to define the study object with which we are concerned. There are, however, several points to be
made about assumptions inherent in the definition.
First, by maintaining that the "occasion [is]...
an encapsulated expression of the shared cognitive
forms and values of a society," one implies a
positivistic attitude toward event--that music is
a vehicle for expression of the larger culture.
This gives dominance to the shared aspect of music
and less attention to existential expression in
the event. Second, by using the phrase, "not only
the music but also the totality of associated behavior and underlying concepts," the old sound/
behavior dichotomy is still present in a kind of
"music *and* culture" rather than a "music *as* culture" configuration. Some other unified expression
is fundamental if a unitary approach is to be realized.
Michael Asch's discussion of the Slavey Drum
Dance further introduced ethnomusicologists to
"musical event." He defined it as

> the perceived focus, purpose and observed behavior
> associated with the actual performance of a com-
> position during a musical occasion (1975:245).

His definition avoided the sound/behavior split.
His application of "event" to data, however,
raised some confusion, for he distinguished "event"
as a subcategory of rather than synonymous with
"occasion." He made the distinction by saying

that, "songs performed during an occasion, although sharing certain contextual features in common, also may well differ in social context in that they are played to evoke different musical events" (1975: 245). As a specific example, Asch labeled the Slavey Drum Dance as a musical *occasion* and the phases of that occasion such as Rabbit Dance, consisting of several songs, as *event*. Such a problem points to the need for a more thorough and comprehensive treatment of "event" and specification of assumptions when ethnographic studies are conducted.

From the literature cited, it becomes apparent that event can be conceived very narrowly or very broadly depending on the direction one' turns for ideas. Some musicologists would understand "event" to be something as limited as a single musical phrase or a song. Charles Seeger's definition of "music event" in one of his writings included, but was not necessarily limited to, such an idea. He defined "music event" as "a thing, a fact, a phenomenon; i.e., an item of given and/or stimulated attention" (1971:387). On the other hand, the sociologist Richard H. Brown explained event in a much broader and inclusive way when he said,

> The very idea of "experience" or "having an experience" presupposes that certain phenomena have been defined as "events" and typified into a "set." A picnic, our trip to France, getting married, mother's operation, *become* experiences to the extent that they are organized in the imagination into beginnings, middles, and ends, or into some other principles of form, cogency, and closure (1977b:154-55).

The notion of event has arisen quite easily in the social sciences among those scholars studying small group interaction. This has included sociolinguists, anthropologists, and sociologists. As a concept it has been part of the constellation of terms engendered by the root metaphor of "drama." As Richard H. Brown concludes, drama has served as a kind of fundamental image for interpreting the world and human conduct (1977b:153). Thus, terms like roles, parts, actors, and action became commonplace. And Erving Goffman's concern with "front stage" and "back stage" have been part of the working vocabulary of such scholars (1959).

Dell Hymes, a sociolinguist, has modified some of of this dramaturgical imagery and added communication theory terms when he says that the communication event can be described in terms of participants, setting, code, channels, message-form, and topics or themes (1964:15). Douglas Midgett analyzed musical events adopting Hymes' model with the statement,

> This kind of approach need not be confined to the examination of speech events, but is equally appropriate and useful to orient a study of musical events where individual performance appears to be a significant feature (1977:55).

Similarly Fremont Besmer defined music situation as an "event, particularly one in which musicians or praise singers participate." He described these events in terms of participants, behavior, and venue (1970:438). Finally, Richard Bauman in stressing the emergent quality of performance reflected the dramaturgical and communication aspects. He noted,

> The emergent quality of performance resides in the interplay between communicative resources, individual competence, and the goals of the participant, within the context of the particular situations (1977:38).

All of these discussions represent relatively new attempts to grapple with event. Further research will no doubt expand and clarify the possible approaches.

In the approach that has been earlier outlined, as the ethnomusicologist focuses at the level of event, he explores processual synchronization as well as reciprocity by the participants. He examines the meanings maintained, created, or modified in the event. The research, however, only begins with the event, moving beyond it to the other interactions and individuals that have an influence on and are related to the musical performance.

As we seek to move beyond the event, we are faced with a knotty set of problems in transition from an individual's subjective reality to the intersubjective reality of many individuals operating at the level of a music performance within a music system that is part of the larger culture.

As Berger and Luckmann assert, human action is subject to habitualization as an economizing mechanism.
Meaning is retained although it may be taken-for-
granted and may not be in awareness. A music system parallels Berger and Luckmann's concept of institutionalization. When a participant shares a
reciprocal typification of habitualized actions with
someone else, institutionalization occurs. An in-
stitution is experienced as an objective fact but
does not exist apart from the human action that
created it (Berger and Luckmann 1966:53-61).

     Following Berger and Luckmann's analysis, music
performance becomes habituated to a large degree.
This habitualization functions as an economizing
factor, allowing participants to repeat past
action. Musical meaning is not absent but may, at
this point, be taken-for-granted. As a music
system develops, the participants experience it as
an objective fact, although it never exists apart
from the human interaction that created it. Thus,
a dialectical tension constantly exists between
the objectivity created by reciprocal typifications and the subjectivity created by individual
interpretations. Both are present in any music
performance but one, at a given time, may be more
prominent in the participants' awareness.

     At the level of music system, there is concern
with the objectivity of shared knowledge. But
this knowledge is subject to maintenance and
change by individual interpretation. Because *music
is a social product* from a certain perspective,
human interaction that produces it must be considered. At the same time it must not be forgotten
that *music can simultaneously be an objective
reality* created by shared meanings. The *participants*--performers and auditors--are themselves
social products. By respecting these three facets
of music: 1) music as social product; 2) music as
objective reality; and 3) participants as social
products, distortion of any single aspect is a-
voided (Berger and Luckmann 1966:53-61).

     As one confronts the transition from the sub-
jects' concepts to the researcher's concepts, the
differences between the researcher's concepts and
those of the subjects present a problem. Here a
framework is needed that provides ethnomusicological study with guidelines and makes the assumptions behind the guidelines clear. But it is just
as important to search for the constructs of the

music event participants. Blumer maintains that a
concept must first be considered as "sensitizing,"
allowing the researcher to study what unique meanings a certain concept has in different settings
while searching for a common element in all the
definitions. The scholar then defines the concept
as the empirical evidence indicates, only later
developing an operational concept (Blumer 1969:
171-82).

We should consider "rhythm" and "timbre," for
example, as sensitizing concepts--working ideas to
be modified as the research warrants. If the
ethnomusicologist initially assumes that rhythm is
a valid, shared idea, he may already have cut himself off from learning a significant, but different system of organizing musical experience. The
questions he asks may be wrong because they do not
derive from the research subject's significant
areas of musical language, as researchers working
in ethnoscience have pointed out (Sturtevant 1972:
129-67).

The degree to which the crucial concepts of a
particular music system are similar to the researcher's varies as the research progresses. A
dialectical tension exists in which adjustment
occurs as the sensitizing concepts gradually become more operational and are defined according to
the music system under study. If the researcher's
conceptual framework can accommodate and be modified
on the basis of new information, the metatheory resulting from the studies should better explain a
variety of systems.

Relevances for a music event participant come
from sources beyond the event or the music system alone. Therefore, research can only begin at
the event, moving beyond it to the other individuals and interactions that influence and relate
to the music performance. The ethnomusicologist
must look also, if less comprehensively, at other
cultural events. Only then can the performance
event be understood in its wider context. Such
study aids understanding of the broader implications of meaning in music.

For example, the researcher can explore the
network of interactions within the society in
which music event participants are involved. In
the present research project, this led to the
study of communal rice harvesting, court pro-
ceedings, gossip, and other activities, where I

was searching for similarities and divergencies from
behavior observed in the music event, as well as for
connections between the activities. The consideration of further generalization to such matters
as music areas and diffusion are problems that cannot be adequately treated within the scope of this
work and thus remain for future theoretical definition and study.

ETHNOMUSICOLOGIST'S PERSPECTIVE

Many behavior- and sound-ethnomusicologists consider themselves objective observers. Yet if it is
assumed that the ethnomusicologist engages in
social interaction as he conducts research, then
the problem of this interaction affecting judgments
must be confronted. The ethnomusicologist cannot
remove himself from the social world as he re-
searches these human acts, and thus he must realize
that the very techniques used carry implicit assumptions that must be considered problematic for
the purpose of research (Phillipson 1972:93, 96;
Gourlay 1978:1-35).

Since the ethnomusicologist necessarily conducts
the study from a particular point of view, he must
make clear the development of his research process.
The reasoning processes should become part of the
evidence to be offered in an empirical study.
Gerald Berreman points to the need for an "ethnography of ethnography" in which

> *all* aspects of ethnographic method (including how
> one selects his informants, how he decides to whom
> to talk, what to ask, whom to believe, whose infor-
> mation to ignore, what to observe, what to record,
> etc.) must be made problematic--be made the subject
> of inquiry, definition, and analysis--if scientific
> criteria are to be applied to ethnography (1972:
> 230).

The ethnomusicologist cannot escape his personal
or scientific relevances, nor can he assume perfect
understanding of the participant's interpretive
process. As Aaron Cicourel, the sociologist, emphasizes, the researcher must be clear about which
scientific rationalities are imputed to the participants. Only through knowing the conditions under which the data was obtained can one determine

what data are suitable for comparative study (Cicourel 1964:57).

All of this underscores the impossibility of being completely objective, and stresses the fact that the researcher cannot escape social interaction. Not only must he make his research procedure explicit and problematic, he must capture the "interpretive process" through which the participant creates meaning. He can do this only by seeking to understand the performance from the participant's point of view. Herbert Blumer calls this "taking the role of the other" (1969:9).

The researcher approximates taking the role of the other as he enters into communication with the participants. To this time ethnomusicologists have usually limited themselves to two kinds of data:

1. sound recorded, interpreted, and analyzed according to Western music perspectives,
2. verbal data gained by interviews and observations.

But the ethnomusicologist can move toward taking the role of the other in several ways. First, he can verbalize about the performance using terms, phrases, and concepts in the language of the participants. This, in a crude way, approximates discussion that participants may carry on concerning the performance. Second, he may actually perform in a rehearsal or event. If one assumes that affective and non-verbal communication are integral to music communication, then there needs to be an attempt to understand that which may operate on an out-of-awareness level. Performance may provide the necessary opportunity for the researcher to make inferences about these aspects.

Reproducing music sounds cannot be equated with understanding a code. While some ethnomusicologists have argued that bi-musicality is a desirable goal, only as the ethnomusicologist seeks to understand the codes of the other musicians does such a competence have direct relevance to research. It is quite possible to perform in a manner acceptable to a group of musicians while applying one's own particular code to organizing and making sense of the sounds. As knowledge of how musicians order and interpret their music is sought, the bi-musical ethnomusicologist benefits from this technique. Nevertheless, important knowledge--ultimately translated into the verbal code--can be gained by learning to perform specific musics.

The same is true for learning to behave appropriately as another kind of event participant, such
as an audience member. Knowledge gained this way
is difficult to verbalize in scientific language.
It is what Michael Polanyi calls "tacit knowledge."
As Polanyi says,

> Tacit knowing is shown to account (1) for a valid
> knowledge of a problem, (2) for the scientist's
> [read ethnomusicologist's] capacity to pursue it,
> guided by his sense of approaching its solution,
> and (3) for a valid anticipation of the yet inde-
> terminate implications of the discovery arrived at
> in the end (1966:24).

Such knowing involves the fact that the particulars
sought after are out-of-awareness. We know them,
but do not attend to them. Rather, we attend to a
larger whole connecting the particulars in ways we
cannot specify (Polanyi 1966:24).

The differences in relevances between the ethnomusicologist and participant can provide some information when carefully employed. That is, in seeking
to take the role of the other, the ethnomusicologist
may experience certain out-of-awareness particulars
that are only tacit for the participant. He may reveal implicit knowledge, testing whether it is part
of the meaning participants create. The ethnomusicologist must be especially careful to ascertain
whether he has brought to awareness tacit knowledge
or whether he has imputed a meaning derived from
another.

Western musicologists have written little about
the tacit knowledge of performance. Few have tried
to make music communication at the non-reflective
level problematic in order to force the participants to bring it into consciousness and to explain
it. Blacking, however, used this sort of technique
in attempting to learn to sing and play Venda
music. He made his performances problematic by deliberately altering elements of the music.

> When I first learned to sing a particular Venda
> children's song, the Venda told me that I was doing
> well, but that I sang like a Tsonga, who were their
> neighbors to the south. I sang all the word-phrases
> to the melody of the first and I thought that my
> fault lay in the pitch of my intervals. When I even-
> tually realized that the melody should vary, they

accepted my performance as truly Venda even if I
deliberately sang out of tune. I therefore learned
that the pattern of the intervals is considered
more important than their exact pitch...(1973:214).

This concern for understanding the performer's
perspective functions to reduce the number of
inferential steps. The participants create first-
order constructs through the interpretive process.
The ethnomusicologist makes the inferences from
the interaction upon which the interpretation is
based. The closer he can come to entering the
particular interaction through observation or
participation, the fewer steps of inference are
necessary. Therefore, less probability of error
in analysis exists (Phillips 1971:1-11). Richard
H. Brown concludes,

It is not a matter of the sociologist's [read ethnomusicologist's] *symbolic* constructs as against a
concrete social reality; rather his typifications
are typifications of what the *actor* has typified....
His self-reflection on his own process of concept
formation, instead of removing bias should remain
in dialectical tension with his study of the actor's
formation of concepts in everyday life (1977a:85).

MEDIA AND THE RESEARCH PERSPECTIVE

Since no respectable ethnomusicologist conducts
a study without technological media, the relation
of these media to the present conceptual framework
needs to be considered. In this discussion a research medium is any agency, device, or means by
which information can be collected, encoded, stored,
retrieved, and retransmitted.[5] Following Nauta, the
term "information" signifies only potential information, which is thus still subject to the individual interpretive process (1972:165-66; Spradley
1970).
Media, therefore, include not only the usual devices such as tape recorders, cameras, and videotape recorders, but field notes, sketches, and maps.
Even artifacts such as musical instruments, if used
in an interview situation to recall an event or to
stimulate interpretation, can be considered as
media.
Taking the definition further, the ultimate

medium is the human being, a medium prior to all
others. For the human mediates all information.
He collects, encodes, and stores information, but
with an important added dimension: he interprets
and assigns meaning to the information. As the
situation changes, these interpretations may also
change. The ethnomusicologist, as well as the
music event participants, can be considered as a
mediator of information and thus a special kind of
medium. The question then becomes not whether one
uses media in research, but rather which media are
to be employed and for what reason.

If humans operate these machines, and humans
analyze the data they collect, then the implements
can be no more objective than the users. Tape
recorders have sometimes been embued with the
capacity to "hear more things better" than the
ethnomusicologist. While appearing a plausible
conclusion, it is not, for a tape recording of an
event merely allows multiple opportunities to per-
ceive and interpret the performance using the
medium as an information storage and playback device. Technological devices do not, in general,
hear better than the human ear, and therefore,
the previously stated need for the ethnomusicologist to be explicit about the research procedure
also obtains in regard to using media. The assumption that media are objective is untenable.
The ethnomusicologist must specify the decisions
made regarding any medium's use and how data are
collected with it.

Media, in addition to offering flexible information storage possibilities, allow for manipulating and restructuring the temporal dimension
of the encoded information. A researcher can
expand the time in which an event occurs as in a
frame-by-frame analysis of a dance film, or he may
condense time using a videotape recorder's fast
forward and rewind speeds. Skipping around in
field notes or summarizing them before an interview
are other ways of condensing time.

Rather than increased precision, a special kind
of distortion can be introduced in this time manipulation. When, for example, the ethnomusicologist
does frame-by-frame or slow motion analysis of
videotape, the viewers in this new situation sometimes create meanings that did not exist for the
original participants. This can also happen when
music is transcribed from tape at one-half or one-

quarter the original speed. In both cases, viewers
or auditors may make discriminations the participants did not conceive in the original temporal
construction. This does not argue against such
manipulation, only the necessity of specifying the
nature of the manipulation, for in altering the
time, the researcher may bring into awareness an
aspect previously known only tacitly.

MUSIC TRANSCRIPTION

Transcription, for the purpose of analyzing
music sound, has special significance for ethnomusicologists, providing detailed descriptions of
sound phenomena. As realized in Western staff
notation, they describe some sound dimensions more
adequately than others.

Dance choreologists and specialists have also
developed fairly elaborate systems for notating
body movement. Anya P. Royce identifies three
leading systems as Labanotation, Benesh notation,
and Effort-shape notation (1977:17-63). Yet the
systems for sound and movement notation are seldom
used in conjunction with one another. The attempt
to join them is a difficult one, for most ethnomusicologists do not have the training necessary to
use them with ease. Since sound and movement are
conceptually integral parts of Kpelle performances,
it is difficult to use two separate systems of
transcription and maintain the sense of unity.

The transcriptions offered in this study reflect
the inherent limitations of the present transcription and ethnomusicology training systems. Nevertheless, they describe certain phenomena more adequately than does verbal description.

The transcriptions presented here have been made
on the basis of certain assumptions. They are spe-
cified in order to clarify their utility for the
study:

1. *The staff notation of transcription for music
sound notates the pitch and rhythmic aspects more
adequately than those of timbre and dynamics.*
2. *Pitches that do not belong to the Western
tempered octave must always be indicated as altered pitches since the system does not provide
adequately for them.*
3. *Musical style features such as pitch are considered to be analytically distinct from elements*

such as timbre and are notated separately.
4. *Sound and body movement in music are considered to be analytically separate phenomena.*
Since dance, for the Kpelle, is so intimately
linked to music sound, the verbal description
of body movement that is sometimes found in this
study is intended to bridge the analytic separation.
These problems of description highlight the need for
more adequate notation systems that reflect the
musics of the people being studied.

CRITERIA OF VALIDITY

An ethnomusicologist's conceptual framework, as
well as the research methods and techniques deriving
from it, should be subjected to established criteria
for considering validity. Alfred Schutz (as interpreted by Phillipson) offers the following criteria
among others as necessary for constructing and
evaluating social scientific models. A model must
at least meet the test of
1. *logical consistency*--following the principles
of formal logic.
2. *subjective interpretation*--building in the
possibility of referring to all kinds of human
action or its result in terms of the subjective
meaning for the actor (Phillipson 1972:149-50).
Howard Becker counters criticism that the field
situation is uncontrolled by contending that a researcher in a "natural" interaction situation is
more likely to be observing participants operating
under at least some of the situational constraints
the researcher wishes to observe than a researcher
in a controlled experimental situation (1970:40-45).
Another criticism of studying interaction centers
on the fact that participants continually make new
interpretations when questioned about a single interaction situation. Cicourel found this to be the
case when people viewed videotapes of interaction
in which they had participated. But he points out
that we cannot simply assume that they are contra-
dicting themselves. Rather, this changing interpretation is often due to the vast amount of potential information generated in an interaction, much
more information than a participant can consciously
verbalize at any one time (1973:127-28).
The approach of studying music events explored
here grounds ethnomusicological research in empiric

reality.   The basic unit of study is the music
event, that interaction from which participants derive meaning.   Studying music processually is accomplished by analyzing the transmission and reception components of the interpretive process.   In
this approach, the researcher is viewed as a subjective participant.   Although his relevances differ
from those of the participants, he must participate
in the social process to make inferences that are
significant about the participant's subjective
reality.   The approach attempts to account for meaning, through study of music process, approaching the
sound and behavior components at corresponding
levels of analysis.

3
Setting and Strategies

A ke 6a taa tóo, wule-tôo-nuu fé zu ge nî taa fé.
If you build a town and there is no singer, then it is
  not a town.

A ke 6a taa tôo, fêli-yale-nuu fé zu ge nî taa fé.
If you build a town and there is no master drummer,
  then it is not a town.

                                              --Kao, master drummer

RESEARCH SITE

The process of choosing a research site began
in 1970 when I made a preliminary six-week survey
trip to Liberia to assess the kinds of music performance in the Nyãavokole paramount chiefdom of
Bong County.[1] Consideration of the site continued
a few years later when I decided that in order to
conduct a study of music communication processes,
I needed to develop a long-term relationship with
a few musical groups. Because of the time limits
imposed on the 1975-76 research project, I needed
to acquaint myself with the Kpelle people as
quickly as possible while observing proper Kpelle
etiquette. Thus I chose to locate within the area
where I had previous contacts--Totota, headquarters
of the Kwãla-wolã-lá clan chiefdom within the
Nyãavokole paramount chiefdom. This site choice
proved advantageous for several reasons, some of
which did not become apparent until some time after
the decision was made.
Although neither of the two performing groups
studied intensively over the course of research was
situated in Totota, both groups frequented the town
in the course of performing and daily living.
35

While many might question the choice not to locate
within the performing group's home town, the decision proved correct. Politically, it would have
been nearly impossible to develop intimate knowledge of one performing group while living in
another town and also studying its group. But to
locate in one town and study only its group would
not have provided enough opportunities to observe
many music events. Furthermore, I would not have
been able to move as freely to observe many different groups, checking observations I made of the
two focal groups.

Totota served as the area's market town and
every Wednesday became the nexus for interchange
and interaction among peoples of many outlying
towns, making it possible to learn a great deal
about upcoming events throughout the area. Market
day became increasingly important to my research
as I chronicled the many area music events and conducted interviews.

Totota was also the location of the Kpelle Lit-
eracy Center and the home of Zau Gotoko, a research
assistant with whom I had first worked in 1970. I
was anxious to continue working with him, and I
could also consult other specialists at the center
concerning problems of transcribing Kpelle, an important consideration when one is dealing, as I was,
with the elusive texts that are part of music
events.

For these reasons, my husband and I located in
this town of approximately 500 people. In 1975
Totota was the endpoint of the paved highway that
continued northward as a laterite road, and a main
stopover in the taxi and moneybus transportation
system. Stores run by Lebanese and Liberian mer-
chants stocked an array of goods from cloth to
peanut butter, from sardines to kerosene. Several
bars, for which a main requisite was a radio or
phonograph and records, sold liquor. Two garages
repaired motor vehicles. Two elementary schools--
one government operated, the other church oper-
ated--provided Western education. Nearly every
Wednesday evening, an itinerant film operator
showed 16mm entertainment films, most often karate
or American action films.

My two research assistants, Zau Gotoko and
Yakpalo Don, assumed intermediary roles for the
purpose of interacting with performing groups. At
first I looked forward to eliminating their acting

as go-betweens, but I later learned that such intermediaries were essential to serious interaction and
negotiation; their assistance was thus easily accom-
modated in Kpelle terms. Zau continually tried to
negotiate with people, attempting with considerable
success to persuade them that I was entitled to the
privileges of interacting as a Kpelle while being
bound by the obligations of a Kpelle person. This
role changed the entire basis of many relationships
from interaction on a *kwii* (Western)/Kpelle basis
to a quasi-Kpelle/Kpelle basis.

Because I spoke Kpelle fluently, having learned
it as a child, and because neither Zau nor Yakpalo
spoke English, we conducted all our work in the
Kpelle language. It was rare, therefore, to speak
English except with my husband and other Westerners.
Working in Kpelle had far-reaching implications.
It allowed me to reduce the steps of inference involved in understanding the interpretive processes
of the music event participants. As the research
evolved, I acquired a new vocabulary associated
with the specialized area of music performance. My
field notes were laced with Kpelle phrases and
sentences as I struggled to retain some ideas for
which I could not find a precise English translation. And yet, because I had certain scientific
relevances and research goals, I frequently found
it useful to make the leap from attending primarily,
to interaction, to focusing on the conceptual frame
of the research. The fact that Zau and Yakpalo
wrote Kpelle fluently solved many orthography problems faced by researchers and since the project
required transcribing lengthy speech and music
texts, working in Kpelle was essential.

Zau was an older man in his fifties; Yakpalo, a
middle-aged man in his forties. Their age gave
them status and knowledge both essential for acting
as intermediaries in various situations. They
could be reflective about many aspects of Kpelle
culture in a way considered inappropriate for a
younger person. Neither was a music specialist,
but each knew how to ask and search for knowledge.
At the study's end, both remarked on the considerable specialized knowledge they had gained through
their work.

Zau and Yakpalo were much more than simple research assistants. They were part of a set of
interrelationships that developed as my husband
and I became part of the interaction networks of

the performing groups. Our lives intertwined with
theirs through complex events, and as they did, our
acceptance into the clan chiefdom became more real.
Actions and roles we first resisted because of a
single-minded American sense of independence, became prerequisites for acceptance on Kpelle terms.
For example, in the beginning we conscientiously
paid promptly in cash for any work done or product
purchased, but this habit unwittingly labeled us
as Westerners. When our grant money was delayed at
one point in the tortuous process of international
transfer, we were forced to become indebted for a
short time to various people, and this created
important bonds of social relationship. As long
as the debt existed, small but continuing install-
ment payments were desirable, for they helped
maintain this relationship. Even after our money
arrived, we reordered our ways of paying for goods
and services. We became involved in a select but
important set of social relations requiring con-
stant maintenance and negotiation for our continued acceptance on Kpelle terms.

ETHNOMUSICOLOGIST'S ROLE

My own role developed as I explored what was
appropriate behavior to the people I was studying.
I usually presented myself as writing a book on
Kpelle music performance. The role's legitimacy
was underscored by my previously established area
contacts and was enhanced by the commercial recording issued as a result of the 1970 field
trip (Stone and Stone 1972). The copies of the
disc that I brought back and gave to performers
became widely known. Frequently played with
pride in the local bars, they represented for
many the first time Kpelle people had heard or
owned a commercial recording of their own music.
I de-emphasized in my relations the fact that
I was a woman, and a relatively young one at that,
for I was seeking knowledge not generally appropriate to someone my age. Since I was probing for
ideas within the male as well as female domains of
behavior, I presented myself as a writer and was
usually accepted as somewhat of an anomaly, for
no Kpelle role could entirely account for what I
was doing and the way in which I was doing it. As
I gained insight into performance, I was better

able to define situations about which I sought
knowledge. By giving interview participants clues
about what I knew, I enabled them to respond
appropriately to the specialized area of knowledge
I had introduced.

During the course of field research, I attempted
to move gradually from the role of observer to that
of participant-observer, but I only attempted the
latter role after I had gained minimal knowledge of
what the appropriate behavior was in a given situation. Only then could my actions begin to approximate a Kpelle audience participant's actions.

My behavior was oriented primarily toward the
performing groups I was studying. From them, a
network of acquaintances developed, though the two
groups remained the focal point. I wanted to know
how the group members interacted in music events
and where these interactions led beyond the music
events. Thus I not only observed music events,
but court litigations, farm clearing, and a host
of other activities.

Several important requisites were essential in
developing my role as a researcher of Kpelle music
performance. First, I needed to understand the
negotiation of meaning that is explicitly part of
most Kpelle situations. The participants' skill
in speaking largely accounts for the way a situation is defined, and it is incumbent upon the
researcher to realize this. Certain situations
always require active and explicit negotiation,
and only through participation can one begin to
communicate adequately. Second, I needed to exhibit verbal competence. Since the Kpelle place
high value on speaking, the researcher must be
fluent in the language as well as skilled in certain interactional nuances. I soon learned that
respect came only after my demonstration of knowledge of these subtleties. For example, a token
gift to performers with an elaborate speech was
more genuinely appreciated than a large gift with
no speech. Third, I needed continually to exchange tokens as a way of constructing everyday
and ritual interaction. A Kpelle gives and receives
tokens constantly, especially in formalized interaction, and these tokens are necessary cues for
continuing that interaction. For example, if a
Kpelle goes to a funeral gathering, he approaches
the mourners and offers a small coin to the head
mourner. With the offering the visitor says, "Kwa

gbulôn kâa a nẽi" (We tie ourselves to you with a
dime). After initial acceptance and thanks a further token is immediately offered by the visitor
with a phrase such as "Tuma ká tí kwa bu zaai mẽi"
(Here are leaves we are putting on the corpse).
When the visitor departs, he gives a leave-taking
token known as *páma-sen*. In turn, he receives verbal tokens after each gift in the form of thanks
expressed by the head mourner, speaking for the
group.

PERFORMING GROUPS

For my in-depth research, I selected two performing groups: one group which was based in a town
characterized by political structures considered to
be "traditional," and governed by a town chief, and
one group which lived in a rubber camp, a settlement for people who leave their home towns for wage
work and who are usually not governed by a town
chief. Local people considered both groups competent but not exceptional in their performance
skill. The particular groups were selected for
their typicality, their accessibility for research,
and in the case of the Gbeyîlataa group, previous
study of the ensemble.
The first group's residence was Gbeyîlataa, a
town one hour's walk from Totota and the main
highway; I had first studied them in 1970. Their
music performance events centered around the instruments *fêli*, a goblet-shaped drum, hand beaten
by the master drummer, and *gbùn-gbùn*, a stick-
beaten cylindrical drum. The master drummer, Kao,
had left the town after 1970 because of a dispute
and had been replaced by his former apprentice,
Nyai-lá Saki Gbon-pîlan. A young *gbùn-gbùn* player,
Kpanâ-lon, had moved to town and had become a popular vocal soloist as well. Girls who had been
young dancers, newly returned from the Sande
society, were now mature female performers.
The ensemble played for town events: births,
Poro and Sande activities, death, and year-cycle
celebrations, and traveled to neighboring towns
upon invitation. Group members participated in a
single work cooperative during the bush clearing
season, employing music to assist difficult labor.
In this situation, Nyai-lá the master drummer
played a one-slit log idiophone (*kóno*), and a chorus

member, Saki Dân played another *kóno*; Kpanâ-lon sang
in the ensemble, having no special role in this context.

During the research project, Taatîi, the town
chief, governed the town, supported by the quarter
chiefs. The music ensemble included a *pêle-kalon*
(performance chief) who worked with the town's
political leaders, fitting performances into other
interactions occurring within the town.

The ensemble members were slash-and-burn rice
cultivators. The men cleared and burned the brush
for farms. The women planted and usually harvested
the crop. Some people also raised cassava, cocoa,
coffee, peanuts, sugar cane, rubber, and assorted
garden produce for cash crops. Many individuals
attended the weekly market in Totota, buying and
selling goods.

A few part-time ensemble members were considered
important participants despite their residence outside of Gbeyîlataa. These members included Leepôlu,
a hospital orderly, who worked in Monrovia, and
Kpetê who worked in the German rubber concession
about thirty miles south of Totota. Both men had
wives and children living in Gbeyîlataa. After
being paid, these men returned at the end of the
month, bringing ideas and money for the ensemble.
The contact of Gbeyîlataa people with changing
Western ideas and technology depended, in part,
upon these migrants.

Attending the weekly market and traveling also
extended such contact for Gbeyîlataa residents. As
a result, many of the houses had corrugated iron
roofs though neither a motor vehicle road nor elec-
tric current reached the town. Several townspeople
owned transistor radios and cassette tape players,
and at least one battery-operated phonograph played
the popular dance music of both West and East
Africa, the latter referred to as "Nairobi records."

The second focal performing ensemble resided in
one of the numerous rubber camps that have developed
along or close to the main highway. I chose the
Noni group from several rubber camp groups because
they offered the best possibility for observation
and because the group members were receptive to
such in-depth study. This ensemble's permanent
core was made up of Moses Noni, the *fêli* player and
main vocalist, and his friend John Noni, the *gbùn-
gbùn* player and supporting singer. Of these two
key individuals, Moses was considered the "star"

Plate 1.   Noni group.   John playing *gbùⁿ-gbùⁿ*, Moses
playing *fêli*.

Plate 2. Noni group performing in Donketaa.

Plate 3.   Gbeyîlataa group.   Nyai-lá playing *fèli*, Kpaná-loŋ
            playing *gbùŋ-gbùŋ*.

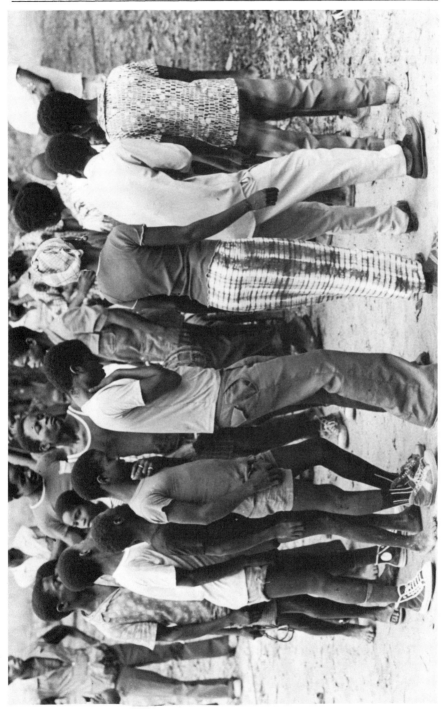

Plate 4. Gbeyîlataa group performing wheel dance.

singer. A changing group of associates learned the
chorus parts for the performances. The Noni ensemble performed in rubber camps and Kpelle towns by
invitation.

The two Nonis were unrelated, coming from neighboring towns. Moses was born in Gbawonma, a town
several hours walk from Donketaa, the rubber camp,
while John came from Disayêei, a small town fifteen
minutes walk west of Totota. Their ensemble had
been performing since 1974 when the two men met.
By that time Moses had already sung alone for three
years, while John had achieved local fame as a soc-
cer player. The two men had attended elementary
schools in Totota and neighboring towns, and both
spoke fluent English. By virtue of their Western
education, they held jobs as clerks for the rubber
farm.

When I began observing this ensemble, its members lived in Donketaa, a four-house rubber camp on
the main road south of Salala, fifteen miles south
of Totota. Donketaa had no town chief or political
structure typical of an established town, and furthermore, the Nonis had no performance chief who
related to any other political body. However, because the group lived within Dinintaa clan chiefdom
it was subject to the rules of the Nyãavokole paramount chiefdom. During the course of the project,
the Nonis moved to a number of other places, including a highway construction camp north of Totota
and Bong Mine, an iron ore camp southwest of
Totota.

The Noni group's song texts were in Kpelle, but
the structure of the music, including the performing style by the drummers, derived from the East
African "Nairobi records," as well as the Liberian
urban music of Mole Dole and others.

The Nonis provided a fascinating example of
performers attempting to remain firmly "Kpelle"
while offering elements of the Western music they
heard. They incorporated dance movements from
established Kpelle dance, as well as Western dances
such as the "bump" and "dump the boat."

The two ensembles were not directly acquainted,
but the young teenagers in Gbeyîlataa knew the Nonis
and both admired and imitated their singing style in
their own performances. When those young people
came to our house, they preferred viewing videotapes of the Nonis. Middle-aged and older Kpelle
people, however, did not think the incorporation of

Western aspects produced the best Kpelle music, despite the fact that the Nonis represented a proliferating type of group, commanding a wide audience in Liberia today.

STRATEGIES OF RESEARCH

The specific strategies developed during fieldwork were designed to gain in-depth information about communication processes within the event and to learn about the organization of musical knowledge within the Kpelle conceptual system.

Specific strategies emerged within the broad conceptual frame previously outlined and the fundamental aspects of the theoretical orientation developed prior to the 1975-76 field trip remained virtually unaltered throughout the study. Many of that frame's more specific ideas, however, were emergent, developing and changing in response to the situation.

In order to make valid inferences about music events, I always attempted to communicate in Kpelle with the participants, sometimes even taking a role as a performer. I observed a great many music events created by the groups under study, as well as other groups. To gain more chances to focus on certain events, I employed the playback possibilities of audio- and videotape recordings.

During the initial three-month phase of field research, I spent many hours observing performance and gaining the groups' trust. I worked to learn the requisite behavior for being an audience member, and I assiduously recorded the words, phrases, actions, and proxemic arrangements I observed. I asked few direct questions at events, concentrating on building rapport and properly interacting with participants. I introduced no paper and pencil, camera, or tape recorder into these early situations, choosing to keep the emphasis on developing trust and ease between us.

These hours of interaction involved both significant and trivial activities, but all helped me to learn to live in time together with these Kpelle performers. I attended funerals, birth celebrations, court litigations, and market negotiations, engaged in cooking conversations, tailor shop gossiping, leisure time activities in a gin shop, and watched children playing. For a researcher from

the Western clock-time orientation, much of my education involved learning to live a life centered on
a time system other than that represented by the
clock, as well as learning to notice apparently insignificant details.

My relationship with the music-event participants changed over time. In the beginning, we discussed obvious and innocuous subjects, but as I became knowledgeable about more performance elements,
I gained deeper access to information because I
could demonstrate relevant knowledge and formulate
appropriate questions. In the final research
stage, participants saw me as a repository of some
specialized knowledge, on occasion asking me questions about certain aspects of Kpelle music. While
I was never secretive about information, I always
protected the sources of that information, particularly since knowledge gained about performance
aspects sometimes also involved knowledge that
could be used in social disputes or disagreements.

Research media used in the project included pen
and pencil notes, audiotape recordings, still
photographs, and videotape recordings.

A variety of techniques and strategies were
employed at different stages. At all times I, as
the researcher, was engaged in a social process,
experiencing a role-focus tension. At various
times, I became more or less an ethnomusicologist
and concomitantly less or more a Kpelle participant.

Participant-Observation

Derek Phillips, in quoting Raymond Gold, enumer-
ates four possible roles that can be distinguished
for the participant-observer (Phillips 1971:135):
1. *Complete participant*--his identity as a
researcher is not known to those he is studying,
and he acts as a participant in the areas of his
concern. An ethnomusicologist, for example, might
perform in a music event while concealing his scholarly identity.
2. *Participant-as-observer*--the researcher and
people being studied are aware that both participation and observation are part of a field relationship. Howard Becker, for instance, worked on
his study of musicians while performing music in
Chicago, though he did not limit his performing to
the field situation (1951:136-44).

3. *Observer-as-participant*--the researcher conducts rather formal observation with little participation in the activities of the people being
studied.

4. *Complete observer*--the researcher in this
case avoids social interaction with those he is
studying, trying to observe in such a way that they
are unaware of his observation.

In this particular study, I rarely engaged in
participant interaction of either the first or
fourth types. When my work did fall into these
categories, it was because a few of the participants might not have been aware of my scholarly
identity, but this was certainly never the case
among the Noni and Gbeyîlataa ensembles. Prior to
the intensive study of these groups, I described
the project's nature and scope to the members of
the ensemble in as much detail as possible.

I spent some time throughout the study working
as an observer-as-participant, but most of this
occurred during the initial research phase before I had a repertoire of appropriate behavior
for specific social situations. The greatest part
of my fieldwork time was spent in a variety of
participant-as-observer roles. As a participant
I attempted to become part of a social situation
while attending to my research project, and therefore I assumed a variety of roles, most often that
of a Kpelle audience member. Such a role allowed
me to retain my research relevances while fitting
my outward actions to those of others at the event.
Whenever I attempted to assume some other role
requiring more attention for its execution, such
as a performer, I was less able to maintain research relevances at any particular moment. But
upon later reflection I did find the knowledge
obtained as a performer helpful.

The information gained in performing roles was,
at times, more significant than that gained in
observation. In connection with participation,
John Blacking says,

> The deeper processes which generate the surface
> structures of music will be revealed only by a
> degree of total participation and rigorous
> documentation which involves more than a col-
> lection of documented videotapes, film, and tape
> recordings (1973:209).

Cicourel maintains that when a researcher becomes a complete participant in an interaction situation, he must necessarily abandon his scientific attitude, at least temporarily. Although with intensive participation less chance exists for the kind of standardization which can be maintained using such techniques as questionnaires, a more intimate view of the social process is provided, offering a chance to conduct research in close proximity to interaction and perhaps illuminating behavior otherwise obscured (Cicourel 1964:39-72).

Interview

In the course of conducting participant observations, I noted phrases, words, and even gestures that seemed significant to the music event. I recorded these bits of data in the Kpelle language with information about the context in which I had observed them. At that point they were bracketed information, constituting data to be checked and questioned.

Utilizing this data, I formulated interview questions. While the interview offers the advantage of eliciting information directly, the researcher is in a social situation, actively contributing to the direction and meaning of the interaction (Becker and Geer 1972:102-12). Thus I used conceptual frame elements as sensitizing concepts, and employed appropriate Kpelle words and phrases, in order that the steps of inference could be reduced. By exploring the terms heard, I began to develop a way of framing questions appropriately. This procedure also helped focus the research interview. By repeating questions and pursuing a topic more fully than might be usual in a "natural situation," I could more directly control the situation.

I conducted both formal and informal interviews in rotation with participant observation. After I had developed a group of questions from attending events, I moved to a series of interviews. I questioned persons reflecting a variety of perspectives: performer, audience, and non-participants. I also conducted informal mini-interviews during my everyday interactions whenever I had occasion to meet appropriate people. These included persons I regularly greeted on walks in town, those in attendance at events, and people who came to visit me. I solicited their opinions about whatever problem was puzzling me at the time. Thus, some interviews were systematically and formally conducted while others were informal and non-systematic.

Whenever interviews consisted of more than one or two questions, I tape recorded the responses. This allowed fewer steps of inference, and significantly fewer changes in the replies. Furthermore, the respondents seemed more comfortable having a tape recorder running than having their responses written down. Interviews gradually became more focused and intensive, less open-ended. I became more certain of what questions I wanted to ask and how to ask them.

Interviews dealt with both synchronic and diachronic aspects of Kpelle events and the larger culture. They were synchronic in exploring facets of events: role of musicians, the definition of music, ideas of music evaluation, and cues and markers for constructing performance. They were diachronic in considering general oral historical aspects of individual and group music performance, as well as mythological data on music. I obtained life histories for each of my primary research assistants and the principal members of the performing ensembles. These life histories represented the biography as the person wanted it presented in a particular context. They indicated where an individual had resided, what influences he considered significant in his life, and how he conceived of himself in relation to music performance. In the cases both of the research assistants and event participants, such histories helped me determine their biases and bases for making statements.

I particularly explored oral historical material in Gbeyîlataa where the performance group had some time depth. This led to the discovery, for example, that the harp-lute (kerân-nou-konin) was played in this region as late as the 1930s, although it is totally absent today.

Myths about the origins of music-making provided insights about the connections people make with the world of the spirits, animals, and nature. These myths provided links and connections important to understanding the creation of meaning in certain events. Veiled references to these myths became clearer as I learned the source of the reference

and the embodied symbols. Interviewing, then, incorporated a broad spectrum of formal and informal
procedures, valuable in obtaining both synchronic
and diachronic data.

Feedback Interview

   The feedback interview proved to be an important
technique in the research project. I was inter-
ested in obtaining participants' accounts and interpretations of music performance events. This
entailed recalling a past event by means which
ranged from memory, to the use of notes, to videotape. All, however, had certain common elements
since a new interaction situation occurred and
since a "playback" occurred whenever the past
event was retrieved from storage, whether human
or technological memory. When I refer to the
"feedback interview," then, I define it as the
playback and recall of a completed event in which
the researcher and participant attempt to recon-
struct its meaning.
   A videotape recorder is capable of recording
visual and aural iconic images with far greater
accuracy and speed than is possible with a pen
and pad. In studying communication processes such
as dance, music, and dramatic events, the advantages of being able to record and store continuous
iconic images of sound and motion for later playback and interviewing are obvious and overwhelming.
Such advantages facilitate processual analysis.
   Videotape recording an event collects and records visual and audio information very rapidly,
but while it provides retrievable images which
appear to be realistic, the recorder encodes and
alters information just as certainly as written
notes. For example, three-dimensional objects
and events are encoded into electronic impulses
which, when retrieved and displayed, are only two-
dimensional. Color is encoded as various gray
tones. Even color film and television images only
crudely approximate what the normal human eye is
capable of perceiving. No film or television camera tube can even function at the low light levels
in which the eye continues to see rather clearly.[2]
   While note-taking and videotape recording both
select and encode information, videotape recording
abstracts iconic information far less than the en-
coding of written notes. This is of great impor-

tance to the ethnomusicologist studying largely
non-verbal events, for iconic codes such as the
ones used in videotape recordings are quickly
learned and perceived by people cross-culturally
(Worth 1969:305; Knowlton 1964:455; Ekman and
Friesen 1969:240-43). This certainly was the case
for the Kpelle who had no difficulty in learning
to view videotapes. Information thus encoded was
played back for interviews with reduced inference
because I did not have to recreate the event verbally from notes in order to question informants.

Only after a considerable period of observation
did I introduce videotape recording. My husband
and I made recordings of the two groups being intensively studied, then played them back to participants in the music event, non-participants who
knew the participants, and non-participants unac-
quainted with the participants.

As I conducted the feedback interviews, I tape
recorded the verbal responses for later study,
transcription, and translation. When possible, I
also noted and wrote down the kinesic and other
non-verbal responses. Initially the feedback
interviews were largely non-directed; that is, I
played the videotape recording for a group of people with little or no commentary or questions.
After transcribing several complete playback interviews, I compiled a list of points I wished to
pursue. In addition, I gradually acquired a vocabulary with which I could formulate the questions
more precisely. In later feedback interviews, I
asked more direct questions, stopped the videotape
at specific points, and returned to sections I
wanted the participant to review again. I asked
some participants to tell me where to stop the
tape as an indication of something they felt was
of importance.

In conducting the feedback interview, I dis-
covered that three to four people constituted the
maximum number whose comments could be properly
recorded at any one time. With that number I could
provide a microphone for every one or two speakers
and thus record all comments clearly, and I could
always identify speakers in the transcripts. I
never limited the number that watched the interview,
only the number that were recorded, and the "extra"
people often provided a natural interaction setting
in Kpelle terms.

Transcribing feedback interviews proved enor-

mously time consuming, for pages of data were generated by asking people to comment on even a few
minutes of videotape. As I better learned what information I wanted, however, I transcribed only
those statements that seemed important, knowing I
could return to the audio tape document if that
proved necessary. (See Appendix A for a sample
feedback interview.)

The quality of data clearly demonstrated videotape's advantages, despite the numerous technical
problems encountered in operating a delicate television camera in a tropical climate. The videotape system made it possible to isolate bits of
movement and the coordinate sound, and to enable
participants to apprehend these bits synchronously
while recalling the original event. The videotape playback, for example, elicited the identification of specific dance movements which three
months of earlier research and interviews without
videotape had failed to produce.

After questioning several people about the same
tape segment, I was often faced with accounts
which contained a wide range of information. Of
course, it was necessary to look for differences
and to probe further the respondents' background
to determine why such differences might occur.
Often the differences occurred simply because each
respondent chose to focus on different aspects of
what he had observed. At that point, it was
necessary to conduct more interviews in order to
focus the participants' attention without imposing
my own relevances on the structure of the responses.

Apprenticeship and Experiment

My apprenticeship in Kpelle performance began
formally about half-way through my field stay. At
that time I had formulated some questions that
seemed unanswerable verbally no matter how ele-
gantly I thought I had framed them, for the concepts I had acquired to that point only allowed me
to communicate in the verbal mode. So I studied
the solo instrument, *konîŋ* (triangular frame-
zither), to explore these questions. I tape recorded each lesson, attempting to study the nuances
of the interchange. I also transcribed and translated much of the lesson's verbal content.

Furthermore, I deliberately conducted mini-ex-

periments in some lessons to test the correctness
of certain assumptions I was making about the
organization of sound and to bring Bena-golo-kũu,
my tutor, to articulate verbally certain things
that are normally unarticulated. Thus I altered
my playing in specific ways, attempting to see
what factors were considered critical to the concept of "correct." These demonstration experiments provided opportunities for isolating sound
segments for study. I spot checked my conclusions
by playing these and other experiments to other
Kpelle people in different situations. Some of my
key insights into Kpelle performance came through
this strategy.

   In the context of one-to-one tutoring situations
I had more latitude to explore concepts and to
alter aspects of the music than would be possible
with a large ensemble, in which many different
people must synchronize their actions. After my
study in the tutoring setting I could test these
ideas in the more complex performance context of
a musical event.

   This formal apprenticeship brought forth another
dimension of musical knowledge: it helped me learn
about the role of the musician. As I continued
studying, Bena spent increasing amounts of time
educating me about the proper custodianship of
these competences. He discussed the special and
sometimes dangerous power entailed in being a performer. He discussed how others would regard this
role and revealed how being a musician had affected
his life. While some musicians had alluded to such
knowledge, it was not until I actually entered the
role myself that I began to obtain rich detail.

Classification

   During the final segment of the field stay, I
worked to clarify the terms, ideas, and concepts I
had isolated to that point, employing both verbal
and music sound examples. For example, I wrote
the names of Kpelle musical instruments on individual slips of paper. I asked Kpelle people who
were literate in their language to sort the slips
and group them as they thought appropriate. I
recorded the groupings and questioned my informants
with respect to their rationale for making the classifications. From one of the very simplest of these
sorting procedures, I could see a fundamental dif-

ference between assumptions of Western ethnomusicologists and of most Kpelle persons in the underlying classificatory scheme for musical instruments. Table 1 indicates these differences.

TABLE 1

CLASSIFICATION OF SELECT KPELLE INSTRUMENTS

Instrument	Ethnomusicological Classification	Kpelle Classification
Kêe--gourd rattle	Idiophone	*Ŋále*--struck
Fêli--goblet drum	Membranophone	*Ŋále*--struck
Konîŋ--trian- gular frame- zither	Chordophone	*Ŋále*--struck
Túru--trans- verse horn	Aerophone	*Fêe*--blown
Boo--flute	Aerophone	*Fêe*--blown

Further questioning confirmed what Table 1
shows: while the Western ethnomusicologist classi-
fies instruments according to the construction
materials and the way they produce sound vibrations, the Kpelle focus on the way the human produces the sound, i.e., blowing or striking. This
does not imply that the Kpelle cannot distinguish
the difference between a chordophone and membranophone; rather they simply do not focus on this
characteristic in their classification.
     This classification research strategy was ex-
tended to Kpelle terms and phrases used in regard
to performance, and in such exercises certain
relationships became clear, the details of which
will be discussed later. Furthermore, I played all
types of recorded music samples for categorization
purposes. Both verbal descriptions and sound ex-

amples were tested in the categorization exercise.
    I also ran a simple cross-check of some of these
concepts and categorizations to determine whether
they were uniquely Kpelle or were held by neighboring peoples as well. This was done by questioning a non-Kpelle informant who knew Kpelle as well
as his own language. After his credentials as a
member of a particular group were checked, he was
asked if an equivalent term in his language matched
a specific Kpelle term. Such research quickly
revealed the extent and limits of certain ideas.
It also avoided the difficulty often encountered
of translating a concept into English and then
attempting to go from English into another Liberian
or African language.

4

Toward a Kpelle
Conceptualization

Boo-núu fa soŋ-séŋ soŋ.
A stupid person doesn't catch
  a catching-thing (tutelary spirit).

              --Proverb

    The Kpelle are attuned to audio phenomena in
everyday life to a degree remarkable to the out-
sider. Sound, both verbal and non-verbal, is
noticed, manipulated, and admired. Onomatopoeia
is present in speech and ubiquitous in song texts.
Sound images communicate in a multitude of ways.
    The most general Kpelle word for sound is *tîŋ*.
This term is applied to ordinary sound such as
that produced by a blacksmith pounding iron or to
the sound made by a musical instrument, but when
sound is produced by a person or surrogate person--
including an instrument, animal, bird, or other
living being--it can also be referred to as
wóo (voice).
    All people, birds, animals, and instruments
have voices. The instrument has a voice because
it is personified, but it is also a material object, and the sound can be referred to as *tîŋ*,
especially when the speaker is not focusing on
the human aspect of organized sound. For the
Kpelle, *wóo* exists in the sense of the voice of a
group of performers, of an individual singer or
instrument, or of an individual part of an instrument, such as a string. Other Liberian people
have similar concepts, and the Dan (Gio) even use
the identical term.[1]
    Wóo also means a speech or group of words--that
is, verbal sound that is spoken or sung. In this
sense it stands against *wule* which is organized
sound that exists with some continuity in time to
form "song." While *wule* is sung both by humans and

surrogate humans such as instruments, most Kpelle
do not associate it with natural phenomena such as
the wind or waterfalls. Exceptions to this occur
when the listener has some special power. Witches
and ancestral spirits can and do sing on occasion,
especially for listeners with supernatural power.
Animals and birds sing when existing in a supernatural context or being heard by someone with
special insight. The key to sounds as *wule* is that
they are intelligible as organized. Culture
heroes, such as Woi--the hero of an epic cycle--
sing.[2] Characters in Kpelle myths often sing, and
many of the key characters of these myths are
birds and animals operating as surrogate humans.

When one imitates an action or a sound via a
medium that is different from the original, it is
referred to as *pokôn* (*po* - self, *kôn* - measure;
measure against the self). Therefore onomatopoeia
is *pokôn* as is a drummer imitating the voice of a
bird with his instrument. *Pokôn* is a valued aspect
of music performance and a skilled drummer is adept
at imitating many kinds of sounds. Similarly, an
epic singer is judged for his skill in imitating
the myriad sound facets of Kpelle life in his performance.

All this emphasizes that the audio-acoustic
channel in communication is prominent in Kpelle
life. This acoustic emphasis is also realized in
everyday speech, for example, in the names of certain months in the Kpelle calendar. The month
that coincides approximately with February is
known as *nyên-nyên*, a name imitating the sound
heard when one walks over the leaves that have
fallen on forest paths during the dry season. The
month of October is called *nwee*--the sound made by
the bird *kpalo-nôni*.

In finite spheres of Kpelle life, such as storytelling events, verbal images depict a multitude
of ideas. The storyteller indicates the sound
made by boiling water: *fà*, *fà*, *fà*. Or he indicates
the way a boy runs: *kíli*, *kíli*, *kíli*. He can say
that the confusion in a crowd made the situation
yuu-yuu, depicting the sound of that confusion.
All these terms convey meaning through repetition
as well as timbre.

Acoustic focus on language also extends to music
performance. The name of the two-headed cylindrical stick-beaten drum is *gbùn-gbùn*, which conveys
something of the sound quality produced by the

drum. The "u" vowel sound denotes what the ethnomusicologist would term a low-pitched instrument
and what the Kpelle would term a "large-voiced"
instrument. Rhythmic patterns in practice or
teaching situations are communicated through verbal
mnemonic devices. An iron idiophone (*kone*) player
refers to one of the patterns he plays as *kpéɛ*,
kpéɛ, kperêɛ, kpéɛ, kperêɛ. This phrase, using the
"e" vowel, depicts a relatively high-pitched, or,
from a Kpelle perspective, a small-voiced sound.
The familiar West African percussive pattern consisting of twelve eighth-notes grouped in units of
two and three is conceived by the Kpelle as follows:

Figure 1. *Kone* Rhythmic Pattern

Kone
Grouping
of Pulses

Here *kpéɛ* represents a quarter note value of duration, and *kperêɛ* represents a dotted quarter note
duration realized by an eighth note followed by a
quarter note.
    As a final example, one epic singer, Kurûn, in
performing with the Gbeyîlataa ensemble communicated to the chorus during a performance by saying,

Ɲulei fáa, ɲulei fáa bemeyeɛ.
Let the song agree, let the song agree
    bemeyeɛ (T130.4).[3]

The word *bemeyeɛ* depicts a gentle sound and Kurûn
wanted such an effect from the chorus and solo
integration. To end a specific episode within the
epic, he employed the closing formula,

Diɛ kpála ke, wesé.
Dried millet, *wesé* [sound of the millet stalk
    breaking] (T139.14).

In this case the sound image symbolically depicted
both ripe millet breaking and the ending of a completed episode.

Aside from the Kpelle performance metalanguage, the texts within music events abound with vivid sound depictions. Both the Gbeyîlataa group and the Noni group employed the following phrase, with minor variation, in their song texts. As Féme from Gbeyîlataa performed it she sang,

Kû ɓarâa kpèla-pèlee, na ñei tê nelei sû, nâ nyèn.
Our fellow young women, I raised my eyes to the
    sky, I lowered them.

Ŋei-yâ è pù gata-gata yè gbài-kpàn-sû-gbài.
My tears fell gata-gata like corn from an old
    corn farm (ATR454.3/T51.15-16).[4]

The term gata-gata conveys the sound of the dropping tears.

In performing the Woi epic cycle with the Gbeyîlataa ensemble, Kurûn laced his text with verbal imitations of sounds: musical instruments, voices of birds, and people walking. One of his most explicit imitations occurred in an episode in which he told of how Woi banished a jealous wife to the fork in the road outside of town. There she was forced to make a living by carving wooden bowls with her voice. The sounds of her singing chipped away the wood, and male clients paid by making love with her.

The words employed as she carved not only imitated the subtle nuances of the sounds of fine carving, they also translated aspects of visual appearance to the audio channel.

Bônkai kpolôn, kpolôn, kpolôn, kpolôn, kpolôn,
[large inside]
    kpolôn, kpolôn, kpolôn, kpolôn, kpolôn,
    kpolôn, kpolôn, kpolôn.

Kpolôn fêe-laa.
    [flatness].

Kalû fêe-laa.
Bowl [flatness].

Kôro kôro, mòno mòno, fêe-laa.
[smallness, shiny blackness, flatness]   performed
    three times

Kalù kôro kôro.
Bowl [smallness].

Kalù mòno mòno.
Bowl [shiny blackness]

Kalù bônkai.
Bowl [large inside] (T160.2ff).[5]

When a female client appeared, Woi's wife showed
her obvious distaste for carving for this woman.
To the amusement of the storytelling event audience, she used only one term to describe the carving sound and quickly finished the job:

Kpîtili, kpîtili, kalù kpîtili...
[Ugliness]   bowl... (T163.13).

Children's games, many of which incorporate
songs, also show attention to sound detail. The
children from Gbeyîlataa, for example, play and
sing the following game:

Leader: *Bênen pâ î tôu-kaoi sôn.*
         Rat come and take the palm nut.

Chorus: *Nelele.*
         [sound of rat creeping] (T367).

The children sit in a circle. As the leader sings
the opening phrase and the chorus responds each
time, the players rhythmically move a finger from
the center of the circle to its outer perimeter and
back. The soloist, by controlling the number of
song repetitions, can avoid ending when his finger
is in the middle. This movement represents attempts to entice the rat to come to the very center
of the circle where a token representing the palm
nut has been placed. The choral reply acoustically
depicts the rat's slow, stealthy movement.
    The children sing the last part of the game in
unison, continuing to move their fingers back and
forth and hoping not to be caught in the middle--
the symbolic trap--when the song ends. In this
last part, the words add a further sound image--
that of catching a bird's leg in a trap under
water.

Unison: *Kêi-kêi-zî-kêe, wêrei-kao gbaaɴ tée yâ mu,*
[Bird named by voice sound] hind-leg bone
    cut a water vine under water,

vù-kù-váo, yóloɴ-oo.
[sound of being caught, sound of quickness]

Doo-nûu yóloɴ-oo mòi.
The singer is very quick (T367).

The concern with *pokôɴ*, specifically imitation
of action and sound through non-verbal means, is
also evident. Kao, former master drummer from
Gbeyîlataa, imitated the sound of the *ɴamû* or
spirit of the Poro by making a sound with his voice
near the drumhead. He also imitated sounds of the
slit drum, hourglass drum, and transverse wooden
horn with his goblet drum.

In non-performance contexts, automobile horns
contribute importantly to the total audio environ-
ment. Some "money-buses"--commercial transport
pickups--are equipped with fancy horns that play
a short melodic phrase of several different pitches.
These, as well as simpler horns, are sounded as
the vehicle approaches the town and continue to be
heard until it has disappeared. In fact, in an
oral history account, one of these horns was so
admired that it received a proper name, Te-te-pûu,
and a special music performance was named after
it.

Audio phenomena are focal areas both within the
finite sphere of *pêle* and, more broadly, in everyday life. People point to and label the subtle
shadings of sound from one audio medium to another,
and from non-audio media--such as visual media--to
audio media. Not only is audio primary, but where
a Westerner might rely on a visual image to explain
sound--as in the expression "tone color"--the
Kpelle more often rely on a sound image to explain
visual aspects of experience.

SONIC CONCEPTUALIZATION

To describe sonic conceptualization from the
Kpelle perspective requires that the ethnomusicologist bracket such concepts as "pitch" and "timbre," holding them open to question. This requires

him to step back, as it were, and apply a broader
frame to the study than he has previously employed,
for if he assumes that the Western categories are
valid, those categories significant to the Kpelle
may be obscured. So little research has been conducted cross-culturally concerning categories such
as "pitch" and "timbre" that, in most cases, we do
not know their applicability.

Significant Kpelle music concepts appeared
throughout the research project, but only during
the latter part of the study did I begin to comprehend them. A considerable initiation period
was necessary for development of background knowledge of Kpelle ideas to make it possible for me to
interpret my data from a quasi-Kpelle perspective.

Several basic notions underlie Kpelle concepts
of sound and its organization. First, sound,
though analytically separable from other communication channels such as the kinesic and visual, is
conceptually part of several areas in the finite
sphere of music performance. Speech, dance, instrumental playing, singing are transmutable and
transformable within the performance situation,
and these channels become interchangeable in certain respects. A solo dancer, for example, eval-
uated a particular master drummer's skill as follows:

Va ŋgóo siye a ŋélee.
He doesn't pick up my feet well.

A drummer, in another example, commented on how
he plays for dancers:

Ŋúui a ke mãlai, berei a góo siye lai, í ké nale tí.
When a person is dancing, the way he raises his feet,
    you play it that way.

Finally, someone commented on a dance he had observed:

Mãla è m̃ó tí...
That dance she spoke (executed)...

The essence of describing the nature of music-
event interaction is contained in the Kpelle word
sân, a term which is equally descriptive of dance,
speech, or music sound quality. While we may separate music sound from these other channels for ana-

lytical purposes, it is, for the Kpelle, much more
closely bound and interchangeable with them than is
the case in Western music.

The Kpelle distinguish *wóo su kéte* (voice with a
large inside) from *wóo su kuro têi* (voice with a
small inside). Occasionally, they also distinguish
a voice in the middle (*sáma*) between these extremes.
This concept of "large" and "small" applies to
singing voices, instrumental sounds, and speaking
voices, and the idea incorporates both pitch and
resonance attributes. A large voice is both lower
in pitch and more resonant than a smaller voice.
This distinction parallels Herzog's analysis for
the Jabo (Glebo) in southeastern Liberia. The Jabo
designate a small voice *ke*, the name for a bird
with a high-pitched voice; and a large voice *dolo*,
the name for a bird with a low-pitched voice.
Herzog also points out that pitch is not isolated
by the Jabo from its association with other sound
elements (1934:452-66). Similarly, Zemp reports
the Dan distinctions of large and small voice (1971:
72).

In verbalization, the Kpelle focus to a great
extent on qualities of timbre. They describe a
voice as *toôi* (standing), or *kulâi* (coming out),
words which denote clarity and penetration. As one
informant said while participating in a feedback
interview:

Dóo fé kulâi wén nyti a póri núu wóli toôi.
His voice doesn't come out *wen* [penetrating sound]
     in a way that it stands a person's ear.

The Kpelle also speak of a sound as *nooôi*
(voiced), which implies resonance in addition to
clarity and penetration. Still another way of describing a voice is to say *nóo su ponoôi* (voice
whose inside is clear) which contrasts with *nóo su
kpinie* (voice whose inside is dark). The former
is preferred in music performance.

Lack of clarity is expressed as *nóo gãla-gãla,*
the hyphenated form of an onomatopoeic expression.
Lack of penetration is also labled *nóo kpélee*
(voice swallowed).

Another dimension of sonic quality can be termed
"level of energy." Thus the Kpelle speak of *nóo
têe yelêi* (voice raised to the sky) in contrast to
nóo maa yénoo (voice lowered). This distinction involves dynamics, tempo, pitch and sometimes timbre.

Therefore, if one performer tells another to lower
his voice, it may mean he should sing more softly,
more slowly, at a lower pitch level, or all three
of these things. Energy level also applies when
evaluating a drummer, and one audience member commented as follows about a drummer:

> *Ŋyêe maa yênoo, a nalêi sĩi-sĩi.*
> His hands are lowered, he's playing *sĩi-sĩi*
>   [sound of quietness].

Energy level also applies to evaluating dance movement as when one listener commented in a feedback
interview,

> *Lê 6ê nêi a toði gé gè tĩ góo saai?*
> What is he standing, doing that his feet are dying?

   Another set of terms relating to energy level
involves the concepts of heavy (*wie*) and light
(*fúanoi*)[6].   These terms gloss the categories of
pitch, timbre, tempo, and sometimes dynamics. A
poor drummer may be characterized as having heavy
hands or a poor dancer as having heavy feet. The
terms are also used in a non-evaluative manner:
when a performer asks another to "be heavy on it"
(*nwiêe ma*), he means to emphasize and dwell on the
sound through dynamic and durational accent. A
heavy voice (*wóo wie*) is considered both resonant
and low-pitched, although this designation is an
infrequent one.
   By virtue of the use of staff notation, Western
ethnomusicologists emphasize the isolation of individual points of sound, for each point takes on
a concrete reality as it is written as a note head
for visual comprehension and manipulation. While
Kpelle musicians recognize and distinguish these
individual sounds, as evidenced in tuning patterns
and names, pitch is not their primary conceptual
focus.
   The Kpelle demonstrate a great facility for
multiple structuring of sound. That is, they
appear to focus simultaneously on very specific,
small sound units and on much broader sound combinations. They do not consider one note and its
successive notes linearly, but rather the multiple ways a note exists with others in time.
Ideally, performance involves many individual
sounds coming together as a unitary whole, con-

structed from many diverse parts. A chorus does
not respond in unison; rather, it breaks up into
individual parts. This fractioning includes the
low-pitched ostinato chorus members, *mûu-siye-
ɓêlai* (owl-raising-people) singing multi-ostinato
parts. Referring to this, one informant said,

Nûai di kê fâa nule wôoi mu tèi têi.
The people should respond to the song individually.

Nulei fé kê zuu-oo.
The song shouldn't be just *zuu* [sound of unison].

For this reason also, hocket performance is
much admired and valued. In *túru* (transverse horn)
ensembles, for example, each performer plays one or
two notes that are fitted to those of other performers, thus interlocking to comprise the single
melodic unit. Such complex synchronization exemplifies this principle of simultaneous individual-
ization.

A further dimension of Kpelle sonic concepts
touches on Western considerations of polyphony,
rhythm, and tempo. Two sounds considered to be
related to one another are designated *poriêe* (fit
or equivalent). They are identical, existing in
proper sonic or temporal relation. Therefore, the
term *poriêe* embraces the temporal and sonic dimensions simultaneously.

TEMPORAL CONCEPTUALIZATION

Basic to understanding Kpelle temporality--both
as it exists in everyday life and in music events--
is a recognition of its multiple dimensions. One
idea on multiple-dimension time, as put forth by
Alfred Schutz, is that we exist together in multiple dimensions of time (1962:169-77). In its
broad design, this notion is compatible with Kpelle
thinking, and the dimensions labeled by Schutz as
"inner" and "outer" time can be profitably explored
in detail for the Kpelle.
Previous studies of African music temporality
have usually focused on analysis of music according
to a unidimensional linearity. Furthermore, as
Merriam has pointed out, analysis has been pursued
with the inherent ethnomusicological assumption
that equally spaced beats are basic to music sound

organization (1977). Linearity does not adequately
fit the Kpelle situation, as will be evident when
features of Kpelle temporal concepts are discussed.

First, outer time, for the Kpelle, is conceived
in three-dimensional spatial terms: this space is
created, manipulated, and altered within the interaction of a music event. It is characterized at
one level by the distinction between the "inside"
of the performance, as opposed to the "outside" of
the performance. A performer says, "Kwa lói bêlei
su" (We are entering the inside of the performance). Actions are classified as taking place
inside or outside the finite sphere of *pêle*.

On another level, if one speaks of *ɰulei tí pôlu*
(behind that song) one means either the song before
or after the present song. Similarly, *gorâɰ tí*
(that year) points either to the year before or
after the present year. Time in such a system
focuses not on a stream flowing in an unalterable
direction, as in Schutz's outer time, not, as
Merriam has suggested, on a spiral-type motion that
is cyclical (1977), but rather on a three-dimensional spatial construction. This last concept,
emerges, for example, from comments made by event
participants discussing performance:

   ɰulei síye,
   Raise the song,

meaning to begin the song.

   Íwôo têe yelêi,
   Raise your voice to the sky,

meaning, as noted above, increase dynamic level,
pitch, or tempo.

   Mãla ɰâ têe,
   Cut the edge of the dance,

meaning that the dance should pause with a proper
pause cue.

   Ka fâa ɰulei mu,
   Respond underneath the song,

meaning that the chorus should respond to the
song.

Ŋulei tóo,
Drop the song,

meaning that the song should be sung.

Bêlei é yêu,
Lower the performance,

meaning that the performance should pause.

Bêle-kalou kâa bêlei mêi,
The performance chief is over the performance,

meaning that he presides in the political hierarchy.

Nenî tî wóo su kêtei,
The inside of that woman's voice is large,

meaning that the woman has a low-pitched, resonant
voice.

Bêlei aâ pîlau,
The performance has gotten down,

meaning that the performance has meshed and the
music making is synchronized.

Bêlei su é kête,
Enlarge the inside of the performance,

meaning that audience members should step back to
enlarge the performance area.
    The terms "edge," "underneath," "over," and "in-
side" are all locational words within the event
indicating the nature of this dimensionality. In
addition, the verbs give detailed description to
the action: "raise," "cut," "agree," "drop,"
"lower," "get down," and "enlarge."
    A second related characteristic of Kpelle tem-
poral conception is the emphasis on movement or
process. Movement is precisely indicated by the
verbs in the examples cited above. Dance movements
are also described with verbs, precisely labeling
movement. Therefore one says, *lôkiu pîli*--throw
lôkiu, sokopâ tée--cut *sokokpâ, kenemâ ɓéla*--split
kenemâ.
    The dance figures below describe the sound and
movement characteristic of three patterns--*lôkiu,*

sokokpâ, kenemâ--that comprise Kpelle dance se-
quences. In a dance sequence, *lôkiu* is the opening
movement and may occur also between other movements. The dancer "throws" *lôkiu* as she rapidly
steps out to the side and forward.

Figure 2.   Dance Movement: *Lôkiu* (VTR712)[7]

1. Right foot moves to side and forward.
2. Right foot returns.
3. Left foot moves to side and forward.
4. Left foot returns.
   Sokokpâ follows *lôkiu* and can be repeated several
times within a dance sequence. The dancer "cuts"
sokokpâ as she moves in a circle first in one direction and then in the other.

Figure 3.   Dance Movement: *Sokokpâ* (VTR712)

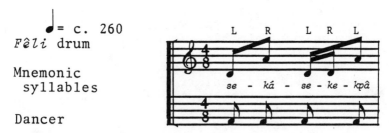

The dancer steps on each eighth note moving in a
circle to the left or to the right. The circle is
completed in one measure. The hands move in the
direction counter to the feet and body.
   Kenemâ always terminates the dance sequence.

The dancer "splits" *kenemâ* by a jumping and stepping movement.

Figure 4.   Dance Movement: *Kenemâ* (VTR712)

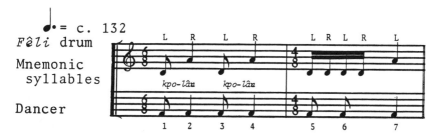

1. Jump.
2. Step right foot behind left.
3. Left foot moves next to right foot.
4. Right foot steps in place.
5. Jump.
6. Jump.
7. Bow with hands leading.

Measure 1 of this movement may be repeated any number of times before measure 2, which comprises the
cut-off for the entire dance sequence.   Once it is
performed, the dancer leaves the dance arena.

In music events, the movement concept is prominent in the Kpelle image of "going down a road together."   The performers' voices going down the *same*
road expresses the Kpelle idea of temporal and sonic
fit.   Conversely, if the performers do not integrate
their voices properly, they go down different roads.
One performer explained:

Nûui kâa fâai mu a nyômoo, ûóo kê lî 6ê pere,
If the people are responding underneath it badly,
    his voice goes on this road,

marâu woo kê lî 6ê pere.
his fellow's voice goes on this road.

The Kpelle describe a song that is fitting together
properly as "nulei liî perêi" (song going down the
road).

This emphasis on movement should not be confused
with linear movement in which one event follows

another in succession, for while the image of
"road" is prominent in Kpelle music events, the
linear aspect is not fundamental. To the Kpelle,
"road" denotes movement which is more than a succession of points, for it characterizes a synchronization of movement among people. Since
walking is fundamental to Kpelle life, it is not
surprising that the image of road is chosen.

The Kpelle focus on time in three-dimensional
terms with movement that is fundamentally non-
linear may be characterized by expandable "moments" or "presents." Within these presents,
people elaborate and build three-dimensional ex-
periential structures. They bring in objects,
people, and experience through movement of many
different qualities, constantly negotiating, fitting, and adjusting one to another, making past
experiences fit into the present and thereby
deemphasizing the linear passage of time.

Kpelle time is like a bubble in that while it
is variably expandable, at some point it must
cease to expand. At the point the bubble bursts,
in a similar way the participants move to another
present in time through a leap or shock similar
to that Schutz described for entering or leaving
finite spheres of interaction. Therefore, life
consists of a series of presents more distinguish-
able from one another through qualitative rather
than quantitative differences. That the Kpelle
are cognizant of people growing old and time
passing in the sense of "outer" time is not in
question. The point is that this dimension of
time is simply not emphasized; rather, the Kpelle
elaborate the present.

The term "expandable" is used purposefully
since, in music events, the degree and nature of
expansion depends upon the success of meshing the
participants' communication and interaction.
Kpelle song texts and their construction offer a
concrete realization of this whole schema of expandable presents. A single text sung by Féme
of Gbeyîlataa will illustrate the point. In the
song she expands the present by juxtaposing different elements:

1. stereotypic phrases,
2. comments on occurrences of the recent past,
3. comments evaluating the immediate present
performance.

The stereotypic phrases, sometimes in the form of proverbs, may be the following:

Ŋá ké a duŋ-kpúŋ-tàŋ-kpàŋ, ŋa sɔ̀o wúru ma neŋ fá pù,
I'm a swaying thing, if I strike a tree its dew
    doesn't fall,

wúru a sɔ̀o mà neŋ ké lî a pú.
if a tree strikes me, its dew falls (ATR454.3/T45-56).

These phrases are characteristic and fundamental to the structure of this particular song. But they are found also in the songs of other performers.

The comments on occurrences of the recent past may be the following:

Ŋá pá ziai sîye damaŋ-damaŋ.
I undertook the trip damaŋ-damaŋ [sound of something
    moving easily].

Ŋá lî ŋá kúla Gbeyîlataa.
I went and came to Gbeyîlataa.

Ŋá pá ŋá wéli sɔ̀ŋ naa.
I came and took a lover there.

Ŋá wéli láa 6a Gbua-pêre yaa-yaa.
My lover's name is Short-road yaa-yaa.

Drawing on another event of the past, Féme comments on an incident involving girls entering the Sande society.

Gbolowa kêtei a yaɔ̀i-ee.
The large uninitiate is afraid.

Vé gbálai pili nî a ɦélee.
She didn't throw the sword well.

Leaping to the present performance situation, Féme admonishes the audience to notice an upcoming important phrase as she sings,

Kú 6arâa, ka ká wóli tôo ɦdoo wule má,
Our fellows, listen to my singing song,

ŋa ke doɔ̀i, ɦge ma yɔ́roŋ 6ɔ̀.
when I'm singing it, I open its net.

She later makes a generalized comment about the
Zokole Kpelle, a group living north of the Central
Kpelle.

Zokole-nai ɓoɓi, dá dí wéli ɓa yíli a manau.
The Zokole are stupid, they cook their lovers'
     food with cassava.

     In this present of the event, Féme has expanded
the moment to include thoughts, ideas, and incidents from various qualities of time. The unit of
a moment consists of both a stereotypic past embodied in characteristic phrases and the more
recent past of specific incidents.
     Within the event, Feme exemplifies the Kpelle
ability to focus on discrete objects that are conceptually united but which do not progress in a
linear order. She leaps from one time frame to
another, bringing experiences to a central, present
focus. A Westerner reading a Kpelle song text may
receive the impression that the singer is using a
stream of consciousness technique to organize and
present his or her thoughts. Of course the Kpelle
can, and do, conceptualize a progression of events,
one following another, and they put it to use, as
in a narrative folktale. But linear progressions
are primarily out-of-awareness in music performance
events. Even in everyday life the focus is on the
juxtaposition of these qualitatively different aspects of time in an expandable present. Furthermore, what is often translated as past tense in
conversation or narration, is, in fact, conceived
as a present tense that prevails until another
quality or dimension of present is realized. In
the following phrases an informant used four different statements of present to relate various
past actions in relating oral history of music performance:

Gbeyîla saa, nyau Gbóu-pîlau a nâa kole, ̀ɛi
Gbeyîla dying, and Gbou-pîlau has now become ill,
     his eyes

     fé nó kwaa kâai, ̀óu ké vȇlii tí siye.
     no longer see, his son takes up that drum.

Many Kpelle speakers also use the English word
"time" (*tãi*), to mean moment, but in no sense does
it denote movement or passage of time. It may,

however, mean coordination of movement as when a
person admonishes performers:

Ka ziye tãi ma.
Do it in time.

   In other than music events, the Kpelle use relatively few verbal expressions for distinguishing
the past. They speak of *le* to indicate something
of recent past--within the past few days or weeks;
nyõo--within the past year; and *wólo*, which can be
intensified by repetition (*wólo, wólo*)--meaning
the entire past beyond *nyõo*. We have seen above
that in relating to the distant past, the Kpelle
often bring elements of that remote time to a
present moment. An informant speaking of the
mythical past simply indicates it by speaking of,

   *...kuwo nua-polo-na, dĩwo nua-polo-na, dĩwo nua-
   polo-na.*
   ...our old people, their old people, their old people.

Even such a phrase is a series of repetitive presents brought together.
   The term for year, *koran*, is a further illustration of the argument that the Kpelle view time
as expanded presents. *Koran* is identical to the
term for the fence which on Kpelle farms circum-
scribes and encloses the farm area. Time, in this
sense, is a spatial area which is set apart but is
not necessarily linear. *Koran* is also the term
used for "ritual," and to speak ritual is to *koran
bó* (open the fence). In kinesic-proxemic terms,
circumscribing an area to be symbolically filled
is indicated at one level by musicians circling
a town to separate the performance area from the
malevolent spirits. On a more specific level,
circumscribing occurs as participants move in a
counter-clockwise direction around the dance area,
thus forming the boundary marker between the dance
and non-dance area, and creating the boundary
marker between the dance and non-dance phases of
the event.
   It has been noted that Kpelle prefer a performance made up of many small, diverse parts combined
into a unified whole, and that hocket technique exhibits this ideal in the extreme. Yet it is more
than a matter of sound pattern A combining with
sound pattern B to become *tonoo*(one), as the Kpelle

refer to the unity that results. Rather, the result is similar to Schutz' "inner" time where
protention, retention, and anticipation combine
to create a unity of various qualities. That is,
at one point sound A and sound B are *tonoo*. But
simultaneously or consecutively, sound A and
sound B, as well as sound C, are existing in a kind
of unity. Therefore, *tonoo* reflects a unity in the
event, existing on various levels and made up of
diverse elements. This performance ideal consists
of creating unity by playing Kpelle cultural rules
to the limit. It is the negotiation of diversity.
The nature of *tonoo* is multi-faceted, depending on
the participants' perspective and interpretation.

The Kpelle do not distinguish this segmentation
at different levels of specificity in a quantitative way, unlike the Western ethnomusicologist who
distinguishes a motif from a phrase, from a period,
from a song in reference to segments that become
increasingly inclusive. The Kpelle use the word
wule to refer variously and simultaneously to segments known in Western terms as motif, phrase,
period, and song. *Wule* exists on all these levels,
and contextual data determines the level at any
particular moment.

The matters of tempo and relative speed relate
to the notion of temporal conceptualization and
are mentioned here briefly in light of the argument presented. The word *mãla*, which means "dance,"
also means "fast." Ideally music, especially that
for dance, is performed as fast as is possible
without loss of synchronization and precision.
The emphasis is not on the quantitative time between drum beats, but rather, on the qualitative
synchronization working toward ever greater precision. It is more desirable to combine many
different parts than to play at a significantly
faster tempo.

From the preceding discussion of temporal and
sonic concepts, certain terms emerge as significant to Kpelle evaluation. Table 2 indicates
how these terms relate to those used in Western
music style analysis. Particularly striking are
the number of Kpelle terms that enclose more than
one Western term. The first set of terms under
the column labeled pitch, for instance, *wòo su
kéte/kuro tei* (voice inside large/small), embraces
both pitch and timbre. The last term in the
rhythm column, *wulei zoo* (song meshing), embraces

TABLE 2

CLASSIFICATION OF SONIC AND TEMPORAL ASPECTS

PITCH	TIMBRE	DYNAMICS	RHYTHM	TEMPO	POLYPHONY	FORM
ɓóo su kéte/kuro téi (voice inside large/small)	ɓóo tcói/gála-gála (voice standing/fuzzy)		ɓóo pílanoi (voice gotten down)	maa félaa (fast)	ɓóo poriêe (voice equivalent)	ɲulei kóo pílan (song's foot put down)
	ɲulei kulâi (voice coming out)		ɲulei liî perêi (song going down the road)	maa tinanoi (turned a-round, slow)		ɲulei maa yee (select song)
ɓóo su pondoi/kpinie (voice clear/dark)			ɓóo zu sãai (straight voice)			ɲulei maa falen (change the song)
			ɲulei see seee gie mèi (song seated on top of one another)			pêle ɓá tée (cut the edge of the performance)
	ɲooɗi (voiced) {}		ɲulei zoo (song meshing)	ɲulei tóo tãi ma (song sung in time)		
ɓóo tée yelêi/maa yéɓoo (voice reaching to the sky/lowered)	ɓóo kpelee (voice swallowed)				ɓóo é ké tonoo (voice is one)	
ɓóo wie/flanoi (voice heavy/light)		{}				

rhythm, tempo, and polyphony. Therefore this term
combines both sonic and temporal qualities into a
single concept.

TYPES OF EVENTS: *PÊLE*

The key to the definition of *pêle* is that in
such a finite sphere, interaction occurs which
points up and amplifies certain aspects of everyday life. *Pêle* in its various forms offers the
possibility for manipulation and symbolic altera-
tion of ideas and emotion within the context of
social relationships.

The types of *pêle* of interest to the ethnomusicologist are those involving music performance.
Some such performance is tied to ritual or religious activities, and the identifying names used
derive from the group with which the music is
associated. The Thunder Society (*gbò*) performs
gbò-pele, a kind of performance with the hourglass
drum (*danîn*). The Horn Society (*mẽla*) performs
mẽla-pele, characterized by performance with the
gourd rattle (*kêe*). Similarly, *sànen-pele* is connected with the women's secret society, and *pôlon-
pele* is connected with the men's secret society.

Some *pêle* are storytelling events incorporating
music performance. These can be *meni-pêle*, or
woi-mêni-pèle. The former is a *chante-fable* and
the latter an epic; both involve narrative, but
the *meni-pêle* consists of self-contained episodes,
and the *woi-mêni-pèle* may consist of numerous related episodes centering on the adventures of the
superhuman hero, Woi. The two genres include
chorus and instrumental accompaniment for the
storyteller singer.

Pêle may also be classified according to the
life- or year-cycle event with which it is associated: *lôn-pele* (child performance) for the birth
of a child, *saa-kûu-pele* (death-feast-performance)
for the commemoration of the dead soul's departure.

Finally, *pêle* may be named according to what
instrument dominates the ensemble. Examples include *fêli-pele* (goblet-drum-performance) and *kôno-
pele* (slit-drum-performance). The application of
the instrument name to the performance usually denotes an informal interaction situation in which
entertainment is an important part of the performance.

ORIGIN OF *PÊLE*

Three major kinds of explanations are offered
for *pêle* origins. In an immediate sense, *pêle*
comes from strong emotions--happiness, sadness,
or jealousy--that must be cooled.[8] It also comes
in a mythical sense from the various animals and
birds in the forest, and details are embodied in
origin myths. Finally, *pêle*, in the specific form
of *wule*, comes from ethnic tensions.

Gé-wéli-wula, a blacksmith and *zóo*--specialist
in ritual and religious matters--from Gbeyîlataa,
spoke about the origin of *pêle* in the emotions.[9]

Menii ná gólon é pílaɲ wule mâi,
What I know about song,

> *è kùla lii-sóli su.*
> it came from sadness.

...*A nɛ̀e í wólo, í meni kɛ́lee kɛ́,*
...Even if you cry, you do everything,

> *fɛ̀e nó í pɛ̀le-kɛ́.*
> you must perform.

...*Nalôɲ aâ kɛ́ pêle-kèi,*
...The man is performing,

> *ɲ̀ti su aâ láyi.*
> the inside of his heart has cooled.

Ílti a sôli, ífa sɛ̀e tôɲ nóno.
If your heart hurts, you can't sit quietly again.

Kɛ́lee, bifôo 6a sɛ̀e tôɲ, fɛ̀e nó í wule tôo.
But before you sit quietly, you must sing (T1-2).

Peter Giddings, a former paramount chief of
Sanoyea, told two myths about the origin of *pêle*.
One concerned a feast held by two kinds of frogs:
lôfo--a medium-sized frog, and *gbeɲê*--a small-
sized frog. After eating the feast, they put their
assorted voices together and created *pêle*. The
gbeɲê sang "so-re, so-re," and the *lofô* sang,
"gó-roo gà-raa, gó-roo gà-raa." The narrator remarked,

Di kêle kêle di wóo ê pú zù.
All, all of them their voices poured into it (T67).

Music is almost always connected with the expression of happiness, and it is also often associated with eating or feasting. In the Woi epic,
Father Spider, Nâŋ-sĩi, plays the slit-log idiophone, *kélen*, as he gorges himself with food (ATR
461.3/T141ff.).
Another story recounted by Peter Giddings concerned a variety of birds who lived together in a
large cottonwood tree. Much strife resulted.
After calamity struck, the birds resolved to build
separate nests. The *yôlaŋ* bird rebuilt its nest,
and having triumphed over the disaster, created a
song, considered to be very old and to be used
when something good happens. The words of the
yôlaŋ song continue to be incorporated into Kpelle
performances even today:

Yô-gèe gèe 6óo
[translation unknown by informants] (T70-73).

The origin of *pèle* in ethnic tensions is embodied in a widely known myth about an argumenta-
tive boy and the Mandingos, the ethnic group known
for trading and related to the Mandinka and Bam-
bara. The boy was told that Mandingos had tails,
but he did not believe it and wished to see for
himself. He had also been told that Mandingos come
to the market before anyone else. There they sat
on their tails, waiting for others to leave before
getting up at the end of the day. The boy climbed
a *pili* tree and sat watching the Mandingos. When
they got up at the end of the day, he saw their
tails and could not stifle a shout of amazement.
With that, one of the Mandingos snapped his fingers
at the boy, casting a spell that fastened him to
the tree forever. His only expression came in
songs that resulted whenever a leaf fell from the
tree. If one leaf fell, a new song had come to
all peoples. The number of leaves falling in a
particular year symbolized the number of songs
created (T74-75, 87-89).

PARTICIPANTS

The people who interact in Kpelle music events
do so in hierachical, interdependent ways.
Ideally, for every participant role a reciprocal
counter-role exists. It is only through understanding these roles that one can begin to understand how participants relate to one another in
pêle. In the reciprocal pairing of participants,
one member of relatively high status who is entitled to create and manipulate *sâŋ*, is assisted
by another performer of relatively lower status.

A vocal soloist (*wule-tóo-nuu*) who is entitled
and expected to manipulate *sâŋ*, is balanced by a
counterpart, the supporting soloist (*tomo-soŋ-nûu*).
This part-counterpart relationship is analogous to
that of the master drummer (*fêli-yale-nuu*) and the
supporting drummer (*gbùŋ-gbùŋ-tua-nuu*). The master
drummer works to create *sâŋ* against a continuous
non-*saŋ* pattern of the *gbùŋ-gbùŋ* drum. The solo
dancer is usually conceived as employing *sâŋ*
against the more subordinate master drummer who
tries to follow and reflect what the dancer chooses
to execute. But some master drummers who are extremely skilled turn this relationship on end so
that the dancer becomes subordinate.

From a broader perspective, if we consider the
configuration of participants, all the soloists,
along with their counterparts, form a unit balanced
by the chorus (*vaa-mú-6elai*), but the chorus is
also constituted to permit an internal part-counterpart relationship. Within the chorus are the
mûu-siye-6elai (owl-raising-people); when they
perform, they employ *sâŋ* against the non-*sâŋ* of
the rest of the chorus. In this case, *sâŋ* is
created through manipulation of multi-part ostinato sung as a counterpart to the main chorus part.

Kpelle performing groups sometimes include a
pêle-kaloŋ (chief of performance). Although he is
not usually visibly active in the performance situation itself, he serves as a counterpart to the
entire ensemble in its internal relations and in
respect to the people outside its boundaries. He
settles disputes among group members, serves as a
liaison to the town chief, and negotiates performance conditions and arrangements for the group.
The Gbeyîlataa group had a permanently appointed
pêle-kaloŋ, the second person to assume that posi-

tion since my 1970 research. The Noni group had
no *pêle-kalon*.

The *posîa*, or master of ceremonies, is a counterpart to the performers at some times, and a counterpart to the audience at other times, since he acts
as interpreter between the groups. The *posîa* often
uses a whistle to quiet the crowd, to bring the
performance to a pause, or to cue an audience member to make a speech evaluating the performance.

The role of *posîa* has existed since at least the
early twentieth century, but it is only since the
1930s that it has been named *posîa*, derivative of
the Western word "police." In rare instances, the
posîa has counterparts known as *sôya*, derived from
the word and concept "soldier." About 1972, the
Gbeyîlataa group used *sôya* in their performance
structure, though they were no longer evident in
1975-76. Male and female soldiers were designated
to discipline members of the opposite sex who
violated rules of the performance by leaving the
performance area or by not appearing for performances. In their duties as soldiers, the females
always dressed as males, although the males did
not dress as females.

Gbeyîlataa permanently appointed a *posîa* who
presided at all performances; several persons were
designated as substitutes in case of his absence,
but a single individual held the position throughout my field research project. He was the second
person to hold the post since 1970. On the other
hand, the Noni group included no permanently appointed *posîa* although someone occasionally acted
the role in a given performance.

The Gbeyîlataa group usually performed with all
these roles filled. The Noni group, on the other
hand, focused more on a solo singer with an occa-
sional, but rare, *tomo-son-nûu* or counterpart.
Furthermore, the Noni chorus employed no counterparts. Though the Noni group played both the *fêli*
and *gbùn-gbùn* drums, they employed them as instrumental counterparts to the vocal solo. The part-
counterpart feature of the instrumental ensemble
was not evident, and the hierarchy existed only
in the solo singer's relation to the total group.
Such differences in organization of the two groups
reflected the subtle move by the Noni group toward dominance of the soloist who is a "star" performer. Such an organizational pattern reflected,

in part, the Nonis' conscious imitation of popular
African and American groups.

In certain kinds of *pêle* other positions exist.
For example, in the performance of *chante-fable*
(*meni-pêle*) or epic (*woi-méni-pèle*), a question-
asking-person (*mare-kêe-ke-nûu*) always takes part.
This questioner is a counterpart to the storyteller-singer, and he gives crucial cues for the
teller to move on to successive phases of the performance.

The concept of audience is a difficult one in
regard to Kpelle performance. Most Kpelle assume
that anyone present at a performance is compelled
by the music to become a participant in one role
or another. This usually means that "spectators"
become part of the chorus, singing in response to
the solo performers; they may also perform in a
group dance. The Kpelle do have a word for someone who watches, *naa-kâa-nuu* (watching person),
but they often say that such a person cannot be
considered part of the performance. The audience
is thus much more actively involved in the sound
production than a Western audience, and those
persons who remain apart are considered to be outside the sphere of *pêle*.

In Kpelle conceptualization, some people physically present are considered not to exist within
the finite sphere of performance since they are
not taking on performance roles. The participating
audience also actively and continuously evaluates
performance with speeches and token gifts made
during designated pauses.

People and spirits who exist in other realms are
also summoned to a performance and considered to be
present. These may be the spirits of deceased
players, great men and women, or ancestors of the
participants, or they may be tutelary spirits for
performers who, through supernatural aid, make the
playing of their clients extraordinarily fine.
Not all of the other participants may know of the
presence of this elusive audience.[10]

Such personages constitute a participating
audience because this presence may serve to bring
supernatural power to bear on certain elements of
the performance. They may also audibly respond
to the performance: a *gbèlee* (sanza) player sang,

Gbono-kpatê wée
(name of a great deceased performer)

followed by "Oo," in a high-pitched falsetto voice, indicating that Gbono-Kpatê was making his presence known.

The significance of bringing deceased ancestors and spirits into the music performance is high. First, a whole category of participants is indicated that must be part of any analysis of the event. Second, by bringing into the performance sphere both *predecessors*--people who share neither time nor space--and *contemporaries*--people and spirits who share time but not space--the Kpelle serve to make them all *consociates*--fellow men sharing both time and space for the duration of the performance. Thus in the performance context, the past as well as other spatial areas become transformed to the here and present now. The passage of time is blunted in the performance context, and the participants live as consociates in the making of music.[11]

In performance, those participants physically present often assume special identities indicated in the song texts as *wule-lâa*--song names, *pêle-laa*--performance names, or *sâŋ-laa*--proverb names. These terms refer to performance names that are abbreviations of proverbs or elusive speech with multi-faceted meanings. Moses Noni, as vocal soloist of his group, referred to himself throughout his performances as,

Suai-kokwêe--Bird-that-is-in-flight,
Kpolo-mú-tumu--Cassava-snake-in-the-thicket,
Móyiŋ-pelee-kolo--Insect-infesting-small-rice-buds,
Sâla-kpaa-kpaa--Big-big-sacrifice.

The names conveyed his footlooseness, his tenacity as a performer, and his problems as a misunderstood lover.

Performance names may last for the duration of a single performance or for many years. A person may take the initiative to preserve his performance name by asking to have it sung. He tells the singer what it is and offers him a token gift for inserting it in the performance.

                    SOURCES OF TALENT, COMPETENCE, AND MUSIC

Questions of talent, professionalism, and sources of music are important to discussion of

performance. The Kpelle acknowledge that inherited
talent, supernatural aid, and individual practice
all contribute to a musician's skill. Kao, a master drummer who spent some years training three
young drummers to play the *fêli* for the Gbeyîlataa
group, explained the intertwining of inherited
talent and practice this way:

A nêe kpô tyêe fûanoi, ya pôri fêli yâle kôplîn.
If your hands are light, you can play *fêli* completely.

Kêe, à nêe tyêe fê fûani, na vêlii woo tî gelee lê yâ,
But if your hands aren't light, if I show you all those
   fêli voices,

îfa gôlon a kâpa tono.
you won't know it for one cent.

...Zân kâa kpô nô îkoi.
...The *sân* are in your stomach.

A kpaa kê îkoi-târe, ê tê tyee-kpua kêlee, da kpaa gôlon,
When it becomes your wisdom, and it rises into all your
   fingers and they know it,

6a zân tî kêlee yale tî la.
then you play all those *sân* with them (T185).

Thus an expert master drummer, as far as he was concerned, must not only inherit talent, but must also
practice if he is to become really fine. In Gbeyîlataa, for example, an apprentice drummer does not
necessarily come from a family in which his father
was also a drummer.

A performer's supernatural aid is a difficult
matter to discuss in the field situation. If a
performer has a tutelary spirit, the relationship
is a treacherous and often difficult one, as also
noted by d'Azevedo in the case of Gola performance
(1966:16-26). The spirits often make great de-
mands in return for their aid to a musician, and
most musicians are reluctant to detail their association with a tutelary spirit. This tutelary may
be an animal or human spirit revealed in the sphere
of dreaming, *nyîi-pere* (sleep-road), as contrasted
to everyday reality, *6ê-pere* (here-road). Informants relate stories of people with tutelary spirits
who became insane or died as a result of not being
able to meet the requirements demanded by the spirit.

Songs and music come from supernatural sources, from borrowing, and from acknowledged individual creation. In the last case, most performers explained that they had either heard a song performed in some other town and appropriated it, or that the song had been revealed to them in a dream. The fact of revelation gave a song a certain prestige not existing in the case of a borrowed song. But whether revealed or borrowed, the song only existed in a skeletal form at the time of acquisition. Any good performer, solo singer, or master drummer, built on the skeleton and gradually developed it into an individual creation.

A case in point was the *koli-gón-són-pele*, an entire performance developed by the Gbeyîlataa ensemble during the research period. A short time before the research began Kpanâ-lon, the male vocalist and *gbùn-gbùn* player, had come to live in Gbeyîlataa, bringing a number of songs he knew, including "Koli-gón-són." During a period of slightly more than a year, the performers created a more and more elaborated song structure. At one point, dance was added. Later, naturally occurring pieces of dried wood were incorporated as dance objects and as symbols of various parts of the *koli-gón-són* theme. Finally, a sub-group of the Gbeyîlataa group became known as *koli-gón-són* performers, and they developed costumes. The original borrowing was a skeletal song that later developed into a whole performance genre over a period of fourteen months. Many participants contributed acts of individual creativity at each successive performance.

In considering professionalism, the ethnomusicologist must evaluate the Kpelle concept regarding musical competence. If a criteria of professionalism is that the performers gain their entire economic support from music, then few Kpelle, indeed, would be judged as professionals, for almost all Kpelle performers either grow rice in a slash-and-burn agricultural system or work as wage laborers (Gibbs 1965:200). In judging competence, the Kpelle employ categories of musician proficiency that are neither rigid nor graded.

First, the Kpelle speak about people who play for informal entertainment: such persons exhibit only minimal competence. Second, proper performers achieve a state of competence that puts them in demand in neighboring towns. These are termed

pêle-kê-6êlai (performance-making-people) and they
are the equivalent of professionals. Both the
Gbeyîlataa and the Noni groups met this criterion.

   The third Kpelle category of performer does not
seem to fit any of the members of the two groups;
this is *loii-pêle-kê-6êlai* (land-performance-
making-people). This Kpelle performer category is
rare today. It includes those who are mature,
considered competent by a wide audience, and who
are often itinerant to the point of having no
permanent residence. In earlier days, such a
performer was often supported by chiefs and
rulers. The title "land" relates the role to the
loii-kâloŋ or "land chief" who ruled in time of
peace and settled disputes over land use. The
Gbeyîlataa group was neither sufficiently itinerant
nor mature to be considered performers of this
category, while the Noni group was itinerant but
not mature. While many young people become involved in performance, most solo singers, dancers,
and instrumentalists relinquish performance roles
to younger people at middle age. Those who continue performing may qualify for the category of
loii-pêle-kê-6êlai.

INSTRUMENTS

   The Kpelle consider sound producing instruments
as surrogate participants. That is, they are re-
garded as extensions of the performers who play
them, not as material objects which produce sound.
In certain cases, the instruments are considered
to be supernatural performers in their own right,
causing the human performer's fingers to move.
   The Kpelle classify instruments into two categories: *yâle* (struck) and *fêe* (blown), and this
categorization is analogous to that reported by
Zemp for the Dan (1971:81). Therefore, *yâle*
includes the ethnomusicologist's categories of
membranophone, idiophone, and chordophone. This
does not imply that Kpelle cannot distinguish between the striking action used to play a drum and
the plucking action used to play a chordophone.
In the word *yâle*, which literally means "break,"
the Kpelle attend to the bending of the string or
skin by the performer. As noted in Chapter 3, the
Kpelle focus on the way the human produces the
sound rather than on physical materials or the way

sound vibrations are initiated in them.

In further elaborating the *yále* category, many people do separate the instruments according to construction material, thus confirming that the ethnomusicologist's primary focus is secondary for the Kpelle. Thus Kpelle group stringed instruments together, drums together, rattles together, and wooden struck-idiophones together. In discussing the two major groups many offer a third classification method, the sound's role in performance. Therefore, *gbèlee* (sanza), *konîn* (triangular frame-zither), *fêli* (goblet drum) and *túru* (horn) could be in the same category since they all play solo parts. In summary the majority of Kpelle, proceed from 1) human manner of producing the sound, to 2) instrument construction, to 3) role of the sound in ensemble performance. Some people, however, reverse the second and third categories. Table 3 shows the first two of these classifications; the third is omitted since it is not as salient as the first two categories.

The instruments the Kpelle know include some that are rare or extinct in the area where the study was conducted: *boo*--flute, *kerâu-non-koniu*--harp-lute, *gbòlo*--paired, footed drums played for rice planting cooperatives. They also know and use instruments borrowed from neighboring peoples, particularly the xylophone from the Mandingo and the double-slit idiophone from the Gola.

The Kpelle are much more concerned with sound quality than with the appearance of instruments, of which few exhibit any decorative carving. Instruments that produce similar kinds of sound patterns may have the same names. For example, *kêleu* refers both to a slit-log idiophone and a footed membranophone. Furthermore, the Kpelle often substitute objects producing the desired sound for an instrument. For the *kone*, a struck iron idiophone, many performers use an empty beer bottle struck with the blunt edge of a pen knife, while plastic bottles filled with rice serve as container rattles.

The organization of instruments within ensembles roughly parallels the wider social organization. For example, in a group of three hand-held slit drums (*kóno-na*), the largest-sized or lowest-pitched one is *kóno-lee* (mother *kóno*), the middle-sized or middle-pitched one may be *kóno-sáma* (middle *kóno*), and the smallest and highest-pitched one

TABLE 3

KPELLE CLASSIFICATION OF INSTRUMENTS

FÊE--Blown	_YÁLE_--Struck
Ɓoo--flute (rare)	A. _Gbèlee_--sanza
	Kóŋkoma--two- or three-
Túru--transverse horn	pronged sanza, box
	resonator
Kó-turu--war horn	
	B. _Konîŋ_--triangular frame-
Kwĩi-turu--Western horn	zither
(trumpet)	_Gbegbetêle_--multiple bow-
	lute
	Gbẽe-kẽe--single string
	bow-lute
	Kòŋ-kpàla--musical bow
	Keráŋ-noŋ-koniŋ--harp-lute
	C. _Fêli_--goblet drum
	Bala--three _fêli_ tied to-
	gether
	Gbùŋ-gbùŋ--two-headed drum
	Danîŋ--hourglass drum
	Gbólo--paired, footed drums
	D. _Kóno_--slit wooden or bamboo
	idiophone
	Kéleŋ--large slit idiophone
	Kpene-kee--double-slit idi-
	ophone
	Kone--iron idiophone
	E. _Kêe_--gourd rattle
	Kpe-kêe--container rattle
	Wéleŋ--leg bells
	Nyéŋ-nyéŋ--metal rattles
	Zóŋ-so--leg rattles
	Tániŋ--single bell
	Zoso-kee--basket rattle

may be *kóno-loŋ* (child *kóno*). The mother has a
large voice (*wóo kete*) and the child has a small
voice (*wóo kuro*).

Rattles are added to the *fêli*, *gbèlee*, and *konîŋ*
and dancers also wear leg rattles. The Kpelle explain that such rattles are aesthetically important
because they multiply the numbers and timbres of
voices heard in the performance.

That the Kpelle consider instruments as surrogate participants is reflected in the naming of
instrument parts. The *fêli*, for example, is designated by parts such as the body, ear, foot, and
waist. Naming specificity, however, varies with
the importance of the instrument's solo role, and
the *gbùŋ-gbùŋ*, subordinate to the *fêli*, does not
have such delineation of parts. (See Plates 5 and
6.)

Some instruments are given personal names. For
example, one *fêli* played by the Gbeyîlataa group
was called Nàa-kàa-nûu (Person-who-looks-on).
Bena, a triangular frame-zither player, named his
instrument, Gomâ, a woman's name, although he
asserted that the instrument was not necessarily
totally female since some strings were male and
others female.

Some performers demonstrated personification of
their instrument by communicating with it. Tokpa
Pée-Pèe, a multiple bow-lute player sang,

> *Ŋá nyêe píli koyèŋ su-ee.*
> I throw my hands into the beads.

After an instrumental interlude comprising the
instrument's response to him, he sang,

> *Maa tîŋ aâ tê.*
> Its sound has risen.

> *Ŋá konîŋ íseyê, îmâma.*
> My konin thank you, thank you (ATR417, 422).

An ethnomusicologist characterizes an instrument
played alone as a "solo" instrument. Yet for the
Kpelle, this term does not adequately convey the
concept inherent in a single performer playing an
instrument, since any Kpelle performance consists
of many voices coming together as one voice. An
instrument played alone simply incorporates the
various roles assumed by different performers in

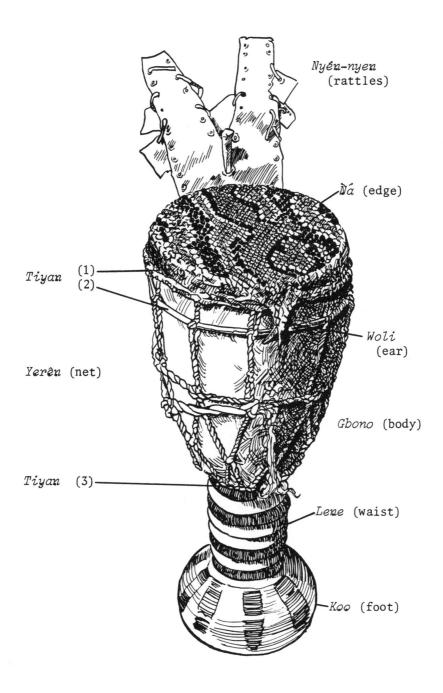

Nyên-nyen
(rattles)

Ṅá (edge)

Tiyan (1)
(2)

Woli
(ear)

Yerên (net)

Gbono (body)

Tiyan (3)

Lene (waist)

Koo (foot)

Plate 5. Parts of the Fêli.

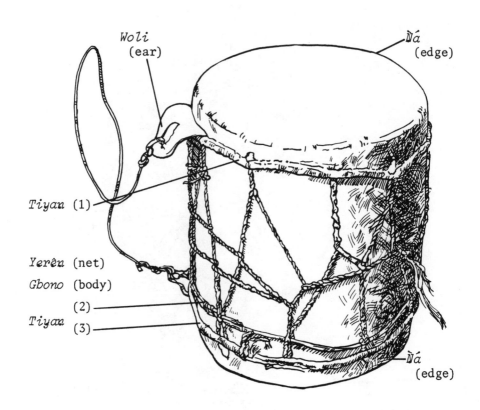

Woli
(ear)

Ǹá
(edge)

Tiyan (1)

Yerên (net)
Gbono (body)
    (2)
Tiyan (3)

Ǹá
(edge)

Plate 6. Parts of the *Gbùn-gbùn*.

an ensemble into a single instrument played by a single performer. Therefore, one person playing the *konîn* symbolically manipulates many voices as opposed to several performers each manipulating one or more voices.

The tuning designations illustrate how these strings or instrument parts are assigned various voices. Two *gbèlee* (sanza players), moving from their left to right as they held the instrument, designated the tongues of their instruments by the following terms, which I have indicated below in terms of Western pitch.

Figure 5. *Gbèlee* A Tuning (ATR421)[12]

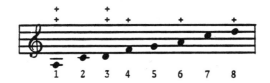

1. *zere-ké-nuu*--praising-person
2. *ñée*--mother
3. *ñón*--child
4. *ñón*--child
5. *vaa-mú-nuui*--agreeing-person (chorus)
6. *nulei-pôlu*--back-of-the-song
7. *nulei-kôn*--neck-of-the-song
8. *nulei-síye-nuu*--song-raising-person

Figure 6. *Gbèlee* B Tuning (ATR412)

1. *núu-kéte*--great person
2. *ñón*--child
3. *ñón*--child
4. *nulei-síye-nuu*--song-raising-person

5. *ɲulei-tóo-nuu*--singer
6. *ɲulei-tóo-nuu*--singer
7. *ɲulei-tóo-nuu*--singer

Although terminology varies, in both cases the
tunings indicate personification, music event
structure, and social structure.[13] Each tongue,
and the corresponding sound it produces, is conceived as a different voice: child, mother, great-
person--and the child's voice is the highest
pitched or smallest voice. Tongues are also conceived in terms of the way the voice functions in
the structure of the music event: singer, song-
raising-person, agreeing-person (chorus).[14]
Finally, tongues reflect social relationship:
mother, child, great person. In the tuning of
gbegbetêle, distinctions between five generations
existed as the player indicated the strings in
ascending pitch order.

Figure 7. Gbegbetêle Tuning (ATR422)

1. *ñée*--mother
2. *ñée-ñóŋ*--mother's child
3. *ñée-ñóŋ-ŋò-ñóŋ*--grandchild
4. *nêye*--younger sibling (of string 3)
5. *ñóŋ*--child (of string 4)
6. *ñóŋ*--child (of string 5)
7. *gbe-ŋâ*--end (string)

The conclusion Zemp draws for the tuning of Dan
instruments generally holds for the Kpelle as well.
The Dan designate various generations of performers
rather than sexes such as male and female, the latter a pattern found in West African groups such as
the Akan of Ghana and the Dogon of Mali (Zemp 1971:
84). I did find one Kpelle player who, in addition
to designating the strings of his *koniŋ* according
to the generation pattern mentioned above, also
gave male-female distinctions as a secondary designation: the higher-pitched strings were female,
while the lower-pitched strings were male.

Personification extends, for some instruments,
to the supernatural realm. This personification
occurs in the association of aerophonic instrument
with the voice of the *ɲamû*, the spirit of the
Poro. For that reason the playing of *túru*, a
transverse horn, is forbidden in a town during the
time the secret society is in session. Furthermore, players who have tutelaries believe that
the tutelary's power resides in the instrument
and flows to them as they play. Such a player
is the only one allowed to touch a particular
instrument.

ORIGIN OF INSTRUMENTS

Knowledge concerning the ultimate origin of
Kpelle instruments is neither widespread nor generally shared by young people, but the older people
know the stories embodying Kpelle ideas of where
instruments originated. The explanations tend to
be based on interactions between man and animals in
the forest at some point in a mythological past.[15]
For instance, the *fêli*, some Kpelle say, came from
the chimpanzee. A hunter in the forest observed
chimpanzees beating their chests as accompaniment
to performance, and this gave him an idea for a
drum; the chimpanzees showed him how to make such
an instrument from a hollow log. He returned to
town with this knowledge, bringing the idea for
the first *fêli* (ATR603).

As another example, the horn *túru* came from the
voices of the *túu-túu* birds, long ago observed by
a group of women fishing in a creek. In a very
interesting segment of this myth, one storyteller
described the people's dilemma when the women
brought the chief to observe the *túu-túu* and pon-
der how they could preserve the sound these birds
produced.

Kwa pòri gei léɲ kû dí fotô síye?
What can we do to take their picture [record the
    sound]?

Gâloɲ é lée seêi, é lée seêi.
The chief kept sitting, he kept sitting.

... Nyèe, "Ka lí daai su wãa tãi ká niɲai veere páa."
... He said, "Go into town and quickly kill two cows."

...Dí ké pa dúu-túu-nai tí fâai.
...They were coming to where the *túu-túu* were responding.

Dúu-túu-nai da faa nô, di di pokôn
When the *túu-túu* agreed [performed responsorially],
   they imitated them (ATR603).

Thus the sound was preserved because the people
imitated and learned the pattern.

5

Communicating in Events

Mǎla-nǔu va tóo a yene,
A dancer does not [simply] stand outside,

   gè nî a mǎla tòn tee.
   otherwise she has broken the dance law.

                          --Proverb

The consideration of marking and cuing illumi-
nates how participants communicate and interpret
references that allow them to enter, operate within,
or reenter the finite province of musical meanings
where they interact within the event's flux of
time. These cues and markers are of varying degrees of significance, some being especially crucial in the construction of the event.

When cues or markers are created and experienced,
they are often part of the routine interaction that
is out-of-awareness. Therefore, the researcher
must, for the purpose of making them explicit,
either wait until they become problematic within
an event or take some action that makes them
problematic, bringing them into the participants'
awareness. Mistakes made during the performance
provide the ethnomusicologist with an important
opportunity to discover cues and markers that would
otherwise be obscure.

Kpelle events center more on the negotiation of
the situation than on the presentation of prear-
ranged elements. Therefore, the activity taking
place at the bounding of events--that activity
indicating the leap from everday life to the finite
province--involves the very real synchronization of
many aspects of Kpelle culture. That someone or
some group of people determines to create a music
event does not mean this event will, in fact, occur.
As an ethnomusicologist, I was often struck by the

tenuousness of the event. A sufficient number of
people had to negotiate the series of leaps that
moved them into the finite province of performance.

This bounding of an event is, in the case of
the Kpelle, a protracted activity, appearing very
elaborate to a Western observer. It involves a
complex set of interactions during which a group
of people attempts to make music performance the
paramount reality in a world of competing realities.
Status of patrons, involvement of ritual or religious aspects, everyday-life contingencies, and the
relevances of the particular performing group all
contribute to the negotiation that bounds the
event.

Participants employ markers and cues for three
major purposes: negotiating to make music, making
music one, and making music many. These communicative devices are employed to bound the event and
set it off as distinct from everyday reality.
Once the event's reality is negotiated, the devices alternately unify the voices as one (*tonoo*)
and make the voices many by pointing up their
facets. These devices will be examined below in
the approximate sequential order in which they
occur in the event when they are associated with
specific event phases.

NEGOTIATING TO MAKE MUSIC

Marking, though most prominent at the beginning
and end of an event, is a continuing act that
establishes, maintains, and reestablishes the
finite sphere of performance. Though the Kpelle
have no single term that covers the word "marker,"
the concept is in keeping with Kpelle ideas, for
there is careful distinction between what occurs
within the event (*pêle su*), and what occurs outside it. The Kpelle also emphasize the need to
separate everyday problems and social conflict
from the performance interaction, particularly when
such conflict might disrupt the performance.

Engagement of Performers

An event begins with negotiations between the
prospective patron and the *pêle-kalox* (performance
chief). The patron hopes to secure the group's
services, and if he is successful, this preliminary

interaction situation prepares the way for the
actual performance of music.

The marking of the engagement is characterized
by verbal exchange, and it is underscored and
amplified with material objects such as coins.
The prospective patron offers at least one token,
symbolizing the seriousness of his spoken request.
The *pêle-kalon* discusses the terms of the engagement with the patron and may, at some point, consult the performers. At the conclusion of the
negotiations, the *pêle-kalon* returns a token to
the patron indicating his commitment on behalf of
the performers to appear for the designated performance.

If, for example, the county superintendent
wishes the Gbeyîlataa group to perform in Gbanâ,
he sends a message to the paramount chief. The
message is relayed, in turn, to the clan chief,
town chief, and finally to the performance chief.
In such a case, the town chief negotiates with
the performance chief on behalf of the higher-
ranking county superintendent.

The engagement negotiation itself is an event
of interaction. As part of the larger event it
constitutes a marker initiating the movement from
everyday life to performance event, a negotiation
focusing on the performers themselves. It prepares the way for a group to go to a town and
perform; it legitimizes their entry and interaction
there. Moses Noni emphasized the importance of
this marking when he discussed the problems his
group encountered when they simply went to a town
to perform without invitation or sponsor. When
women flocked to see and hear him, the men became
jealous, and he was even occasionally chased from
town because he had no one to legitimize his presence.

Tuning of Drums

Tuning instruments constitutes a series of audio
and kinesic markers that precede the making of
music by the ensemble. Small groups of instrumentalists frequently work on the tuning process for
each drum, especially if the lacing strings are
loosened and restrung. The shorter tuning method
involves heating or wetting each drumhead and then
pounding its edge to tighten the skin. The longer
tuning method requires that the lacing be com-

pletely undone. As one person relaces, the other
hits the drumhead's edge to stretch the skin taut;
the drum is rotated as they proceed. This latter
method can last from fifteen to thirty minutes,
depending upon the particular drum. As the desired
sound is achieved the performers remark, "Nooɓi"
(It is voiced). If it has not yet reached that
sound, they say "Vé ni wóo ní" (It is not yet
voiced).

Clearing the Performance Arena

The physical space in which music is created
can be any place where the participants gather and
place themselves strategically in the spatial arrangement appropriate to the performance. It is
not a place used exclusively for music performance,
but prior to and during the performance, certain
acts create that symbolic area and set it aside
for the performance.[1] Clearing out the town is
the first act. While not always prerequisite to
performance, this is done if the group is not
playing in its own town. The ensemble circles the
town's outer perimeter in procession, performing
as the musicians move together in a counterclockwise direction. Counterclockwise movement has
symbolic importance. The Kpelle explain that the
performers are proceeding in the direction of their
right hands (*láa-mii-yee-mẽi-pere*). That is, their
right hands form the visible boundary marker between town and beyond as they move. To proceed
clockwise, with their left hands as the boundary
marker, would mean ill will and disrespect to the
audience. An argument or dispute might very well
ensue if they chose such a direction. These
markers clear from the performance arena the
malevolent spirits that often hover at the edge
of town and may be undesirable in the performance.
One event participant said,

Kwa tínaŋ daai ma.
We turn around the town.

Ku tòŋ ká tí, fèe kú ge.
It's our law, we must do it.

Kwá ge tí a gée ku nyínaŋ kpɛ́ daai ma.
We do it to chase the spirits from the town (T139).

This clearing act also alerts the town residents to the fact that a performance is being negotiated. It announces and advertises the group in the farthest edge of town. Children join the group, and the procession often ends at the house of the patron.

Tokens of Sponsorship

Here the *pêle-kalou* makes a speech which announces the group's arrival and puts it at the patron's disposal. The patron, in turn, indicates his permission for the group to begin by offering a coin which symbolizes his approval that the event proceed toward the finite sphere of performance and underscores his gift with words such as "Ná nyée sée bêlei mu" (I put my hand under the performance).

This initial sponsor token further legitimizes the group's interaction, and throughout the performance his tokens continue as markers that maintain the finite sphere. Whether gifts of liquor, food, or verbal praise, they symbolize his continuing support. If the patron stops supplying tokens, the music may falter or even break down completely as the musicians become dissatisfied. On the other hand, if the tokens are used as skillfully timed rewards, they move the musicians to ever better performance. A gift of liquor (token) accompanies the following speech (act) made by the patron's spokesman. The *posîa* repeats the speech phrase by phrase to add prestige to the communication.

Spokesman:	*Kêe Kiapê nyêe,* Well Kiape says,
Posîa:	(repeats above phrase)
Spokesman:	*Nô surôn lâa 6a Sumo.* Her husband's name is Sumo.
Posîa:	(repeats above phrase)
Spokesman:	*Da yá pú ma.* They put water on it. (He hands the bottle of liquor to the *posîa*.)

Posîa: *Da ma yô-ee.*
                 They soak it (ATR453-55).

Just as tokens throughout the performance mark
and maintain the finite sphere, a specific marker
ends the performance. This marker is known as
páma-seɯ. When the patron offers it to the ensemble, he indicates that the performers are under no
further obligation to him and may leave at any
time.

Synchronization

Making music sound begins with a progressive
synchronization of parts; when such synchronization is achieved to the satisfaction of event
participants, the Kpelle say, "Bêlei kóo aâ pîlaɯ"
(The performance's foot has stepped down). Characteristically, the parts initially enter in a
staggered manner: those parts which have the least
variation enter first. The vocal soloist or
master drummer may demonstrate to the chorus or
another drummer the proper performance of a chorus
or drum part before later coming in with his own.
By staggering the entries, the performers can concentrate on as few as two parts at a time, working
to mesh their actions and sounds in specific temporal dimensions. This synchronizing can last a
considerable time if the group is unaccustomed to
performing together. Such was the case when
Kulûn, an epic singer, performed with the Gbeyîlataa group. He taught them the choral ostinato
parts prior to each episode and waited until a
degree of synchronization was achieved before beginning his solo narration. In one case when
synchrony was not achieved to his satisfaction,
the performance disintegrated and he did not nar-
rate that particular episode.

This audio marker of synchronizing activities
continues as the group interaction moves the
participants to a more carefully meshed relationship. The marking is progressive, moving to different levels of synchrony within the finite
sphere. Furthermore, building synchronization
may recur as new songs or event phases begin,
maintaining the finite sphere of performance.

Gathering of Participants

 As the audience joins the performers, all the
participants greet one another. This gathering is
a marker that encourages the group's movement
toward the finite sphere of performance. The
surrogate performers, ancestors, and tutelaries are
acknowledged through audible greetings even though
they cannot be seen. The solo singer sometimes
acknowledges the presence of these surrogate participants by communicating with them. Kulûn, for
instance, sang,

 Oo Maa-lâa pá a nôo o nûa.
 Oh, Maa-lâa bring my voice, oh people (ATR461.1/T132.14).

Another soloist sang,

 Ee Kamankêe, pá a nôoi Nyãakôi tí-ee.
 Ee Kamankêe, bring my voice, that Nyãakôi (ATR458.1/
                   T272.2).

A deceased chief, Bono-boi was brought into the
performance through reference to his performance
name, Noo-Yele.

 Ee Noo-yele a wôlo lí,
 Ee His-day has long ago gone,

 Bono-boi a wôlo lí-oo nûa.
 Bono-boi has long ago gone people.

 Nûu fa lee nûu taa,
 A person doesn't stay in a person's town,

 Noo-yele a lí-oo.
 His-day has gone, oh (ATR458.2/T276.17).

The invitation to the performance may be direct, as
when the singer sings,

 Saki sére, sére, sére...
 Saki greetings, greetings, greetings...(ATR461.5/
                 T162.2).

 The act of greeting someone reflects everyday
life in that exchanging greetings acknowledges
one's existence. In performance, greetings incorporate specific performer and surrogate performer

identities and maintain participant attention in
the finite sphere of performance.

Reclearing the Performance Arena

An open space encircled by audience and performers and closed off from the rest of the town
is an important spatial symbol of the finite sphere
being created through musical interaction and performance, and thus clearing out the performance
arena continues on a smaller scale throughout the
performance. This action may first occur when the
posîa (master of ceremonies) moves the crowd back
from the space defined as the performance and dance
arena. He says, "Bêlei su kéte" (Make the inside
of the performance large); or "Ka kula pôlu, ka
kula pôlu" (Go back, go back). He gives these verbal commands as he walks around the edge of the
crowd, using hand movements to wave the people
back. This clearing out acts as a marker that maintains or reestablishes the finite sphere of performance which is threatened or temporarily de-
stroyed if the crowd presses too closely upon the
performance arena.
A second instance of this type of marking occurs
when a dancer clears out the performance arena before dancing and between dance movements. People
comment, "Gáa zu kpêi" (She is chasing the inside).
The dancer uses a slow dance step and may circle
the perimeter or move back and forth throughout
the dance arena. This act marks the individual
performer's finite sphere of dance performance,
maintaining or reestablishing it for the rest of
the group.

MAKING MUSIC ONE

Once an event is established, successive phases
are constructed. During these phases, cues are
communicated for the purpose of making the music
one (*tonoo*).
A cue, as stated earlier, is a reminder of a
past act that gives a reference for participating
within the finite sphere of performance. Cues
coordinate the many different actions in a performance. In Kpelle events, cues are communica-
tions between performers which short cut negotiation of meaning at strategic points. In com-

paring cues and markers, the crucial differences
are not so much in the structure or appearance of
the cuing or marking acts, as in the context of
their use. A marker moves the participant from
one reality to another. A cue works within a
finite sphere.

Cues occur as audio, visual, or tactile mes-
ages, sometimes combining several of these modes.
Some cues are out-of-awareness, unnoticed by
certain performers or the researcher, while others
point more explicitly to the communication between performers and are more easily distinguished
within the ebb and flow of sound and action comprising the music performance.

Certain parts of the performance are known and
expected, but others depend upon a cue within the
performance context.

People who can initiate cues are ranked in a
hierarchical order. By virtue of their roles, the
master drummer and solo singer have great latitude
for manipulating *sâŋ*, and thus they initiate many
cues. Chorus or audience members, on the other
hand, have little opportunity to initiate cues,
although in different phases of the event cuing
roles vary in prominence among the participants.

Kpelle performance is not simply characterized
by the cue and response. Rather, it involves a
complex process of relaying cues, which is aesthetically pleasing in itself: each relay enhances
the status of any cue so communicated.

Cues, like markers, are acts of varying scope.
The level of cues we are considering varies
enormously. A cue may be simply the act of blowing a whistle. It may also be the act of pausing,
which is made up in turn of many cues of smaller
scope; the latter process is consonant with
Kpelle thinking.

Cues are associated with specific phases of the
performance event. At structural nodes, cues
coordinate performers' actions. An initial phase
of the event following negotiation to make music
is the *koo-pîlaŋ* (foot-putting-down) phase. During
this phase, the performers' cues work toward making
music one.

Koo-Pîlaŋ (Foot-Putting-Down)

The *koo-pîlaŋ* (foot-putting-down) phase, during
which the music sound becomes prominent, is char-

acterized by adjustment in the synchronization of
the ensemble. Since coordination is often problematic during this phase, it can be easily studied.
In Western performance, this synchronizing phase
is often de-emphasized. Many Western musicians do
not show the tuning-in process to the audience.
Yet in Kpelle performance it is usually an extended
segment of the total performance.

A cue in this segment, for example, is the
demonstration of a proper phrase by one player to
another. A *fêli* player may play the *gbùŋ-gbùŋ*
player's part if the latter does not know this
segment of a particular song. When performing with
the Gbeyîlataa group, Kulûŋ, the epic singer, systematically demonstrated each part, then sang with
the performers until the part was established, and
continued to build the background of interlocking
parts necessary for his own solo performance.

Cues may also be verbal and give direction to
the participants:

Fêli Player: *Ŋulei sîye we.*
                  Raise the song (ATR453.1/T57.1).

Soloist: *Ífe layi tî.*
                  Don't shout like that (VTR705.3).

Chief: *Ka fê ma felaa a ŋâna.*
                  Don't hurry it too hard (ATR453.1).

A vocal soloist, after hearing problems in the
sound may say,

Oo lôii, ŋulei tî e ke a kû woo su kête oo.
All right, that song was with our large voice, oh.

Too ŋâ pâ ziye a ŋôo loŋ-oo.
Let me raise it with my small voice (ATR453.1).

Thus the ensemble uses audio cues to adjust temporal and sonic aspects of performing together.

While other cues exist that could be classified
as making music one, they are predominantly conceived by the Kpelle as delineating music or making
music many. Therefore a cut-off cue is seen as
segmenting the event, or making music many, although it also secondarily brings various parts
together into a unitary pause.

MAKING MUSIC MANY

The cues to be discussed here are those that
delineate and highlight the facets of the performance. Some of these cues are, like the cues
essential to making music one, tied to specific
event phases.

Maa-Yèe (Selecting)

The *maa-yèe* (selecting) phase refers to the
process of employing and creating *sâŋ* in performance; it is characterized by delineation and
faceting rather than unity. The solo performers
are conceptualized as symbolically selecting
facets to be incorporated into the performance.
After the performance ensemble is "going down one
road," this phase can occur, for the ensemble has
achieved a state of synchronization acceptable to
the participants and is ready for a cue to begin
the *maa-yèe* phase. This cue is a proliferation
of *sâŋ* from various channels and by different
participants. *Sâŋ,* as mentioned earlier, is a
multi-faceted, multi-interpretable quality of
performance channels. The *maa-yèe* phase may
alternate with non-*maa-yèe* phases during the in-
termediate part of the event, but since the Kpelle
consider *sâŋ* to be the essence of performance,
the focal point of the event occurs here in its
creation. The whole *maa-yèe* phase of an event or
song presents a multiple image of the idea of
being communicated through music performance. In
presenting ideas in a multi-faceted form, the
Kpelle performance ideal is realized: unity within
the maximum possible diversity. During this phase,
knowledge embodied in the *sâŋ*-ness of action and
interaction is presented to participants.
A fine singer is one who can weave *sâŋ* into the
performance. A singer in the process of employing
sâŋ is said to be "selecting the song" (*wule maa-
yèe*) or "opening the net" (*maa yóroŋ ɓo*).
A cue by the vocal soloist may alert other
participants to the approaching *sâŋ*:

Ka kâ woli kê ndoo wule mâ,
Listen to my singing song,

Ɲa ke doôi, ŋge maa yóroŋ ɓo.
As I sing it, I open its net.

A cue may also point out the end of a particular
segment in which *sâŋ* has been featured. Such a
cue may involve the *posîa* blowing his whistle, or
the chorus singing a response.

A soloist may expand song phrases during the
maa-yêe phase. Whereas in the *koo-pîlaŋ* segment
the phrases are usually consistent in length, this
section may contain expanded phrases, analogous to
the expandable moment of Kpelle time conception.
On a more general level, the *maa-yêe* part of an
event is a variable and expandable, depending upon
the soloist's skill, the performers' synchrony,
and the audience's response.

The vocal soloist relies largely on verbal proverbs and allusive phrases to present the quality
of multi-facetedness. The master drummer presents
variations on well-known and established sound
patterns, varying pitch, rhythm, and timbre. Solo
dancers present embellishments and slight variations of established movement patterns. The *mûu-
siye-ɓêlai* (owl-raising-people) in the chorus
create vocal ostinato patterns of non-verbal timbre, fitting them against the established choral
response pattern. All these actions have the
quality of *sâŋ* because they exhibit nuances of
action and sound, communication different from, but
related to, patterns familiar to the participants
in the event.

Chorus Entry

Cues that indicate to the chorus when to enter
the performance point up delineation and segmentation; these cues are given in a number of ways.
The soloist may sing a fixed-length exposition
phrase so that the chorus always responds after an
identical interval, or the soloist expands or em-
broiders a variable length skeletal phrase and
must specifically indicate when the performers are
to give the choral response. In this case, the
phrases are not of fixed length and choral entry
cues are indicated by descent of melodic line,
decrease in density of text and/or music sound
[called "ŋala" (pulling) by the Kpelle], or injec-
tion of syllables "ee" and/or "oo." These cues
often, but not necessarily, occur in conjunction
with one another, but might also occur with
a different meaning elsewhere in a performance.
Two or more such cues together nearly always in-

dicate the approach of the choral entry.

Both the Gbeyîlataa and Noni groups used these cues, though an important difference existed between these two groups. The alternation between solo and chorus was much more frequent in Gbeyîlataa than in Noni performances. The Gbeyîlataa soloists characteristically sang one line before the chorus responded with a relatively short phrase. On the other hand, the Noni group, with its focus on the soloist, often performed long, extended verse-like segments to which the chorus responded with fairly long segments.

The Gbeyîlataa pattern of frequently alternating parts is quite similar to Kpelle conversational patterns. In everyday speaking, a listener gives more than kinesic-proxemic messages to indicate that he is listening. At the end of most phrases, the listener responds audibly with "m̀m," or "owei," (yes), or "èe." The low pitch is as important as the phoneme combination, for a high pitch signals a questioning of the speaker. This call-response pattern in everyday speech is obvious in the typical opening segment of the Kpelle greeting sequence:

A: *Keemâ 6à ûn?*
    Keema have you awakened?

B: *M̀m, Sumo.*
    Yes, Sumo.

A: *M̀m.*
    Yes.

B: *Bà ûn èe?*
    Have you awakened?

In speech, as in music, "èe" is a delineation cue, communicating the close of the opening phase of the greeting sequence. Such cues in speech parallel cues for segmenting choral entry in music.

Figures 8, 9, and 10 below illustrate these choral entrance cues. The first two examples were performed by the Gbeyîlataa ensemble; the last by the Noni ensemble. In Figure 8, the first three instances of "èe" simply indicate the end of a phrase (marked by a single asterisk). But in the fourth instance, decreasing density of text and melody accompany the syllable "èe" (marked by a

double asterisk), and it is at this point that the
chorus enters (marked by a triple asterisk).[2]

Figure 8.   Choral Entrance Cuing   (ATR453.1)

Oh bearing children is fine.
God give him to me and I will make his feast,
I will send him to Western town, he
    doesn't even read.
He will do his corrupt work.
Whose name.

Figure 9 illustrates slightly different choral
entrance cuing. The first chorus entrance (marked
by a triple asterisk) is cued by "pulling" (*ɲala*)
and melodic descent. The second chorus entrance is
cued by these two elements and a third, the syllable "èe." The third entrance comes after an extended solo passage and is cued by "pulling" and
the syllable "èe" in measure fourteen.[3]

Figure 9.   Choral Entrance Cuing
(ATR454.3/T45-56)

I drink, I bathe with Fanta liquor.
Ah ya Malâa-ke-ma,
I'm the one who was doing the foolish crying,
I have long been a swaying thing,
If I strike a tree its dew doesn't fall,
If a tree strikes me, its dew falls.
Initiates that's the word from there,
    isn't it?
My love leave me alone.
Happiness is taking the thigh from the clitoris.

Figure 10 illustrates the choral entrance cued by
all three elements: melodic descent, "pulling,"
and the syllable "èe." (The "èe" preceding choral
entry is marked by a double asterisk; the choral
entry by a triple asterisk.)

Figure 10. Choral Entrance Cuing
(ATR452.1/T24-34)

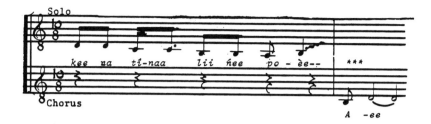

I'm a big, big sacrifice oh,
But I'm going to mother's tomorrow.

Pauses

Pauses are an important part of all music events,
and the *maa-yêe* phase in particular. During this
phase, and at punctuation points after a particular
soloist's exposition of *sâu*, pauses occur during
which token gifts are offered to the performers.
These pauses provide the moment for audience response and help segment the event into many units.
The *posîa*, or one of the soloists, initiates the
pause cues which are usually executed in a relay
manner. The performer's status is enhanced as the
cue relay complexity increases. Such pauses must
be indicated at the proper time after the performer has completed *sâu* to his satisfaction. At
one performance I observed, an audience member
approached the *posîa* and requested that a pause be
called so he could offer a gift. The *posîa* replied
that he could not comply at that moment because
the performance "goo káa ma" (was pregnant). The
segment had to be completed before pausing.
In their simplest form, pause cues consist of
the soloist singing with, or paralleling, the
choral response and not beginning a new solo exposition. They may also consist of the *posîa*
blowing his whistle, raising his hand, or giving
a shout which begins on a low pitch and glides up
to a higher-pitched release.
Most characteristically, however, pause cues
consist of a layering of several cues relayed by
various ensemble members. In one ensemble, the
vocal soloist sang, "Nyee ma, posîa gweli fee"
(I say to him, *posîa* blow the whistle), which was
pause cue A. She then textually and rhythmically

paralleled the choral response (pause cue B).
Finally, and simultaneously with pause cue B's
execution, the *posîa* blew his whistle (pause cue
C). Figure 11 illustrates this sequence.

Figure 11. Pause Cuing (ATR414)

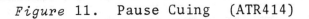

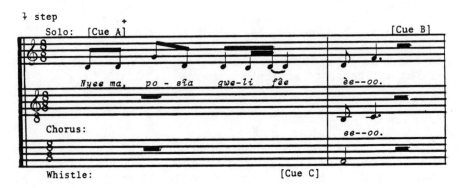

I say to him, *posîa* blow the whistle.

The soloist may sing a fairly explicit phrase to
call for a pause, or the indication may be more
obscure. A well known Kpelle allusion is,

> *Pá berei kooi têe ná tee.*
> Come cut the log in the road for me to pass (ATR465.1)

When a cuing sequence for a pause fails, the situation becomes problematic and can be informative.
In one Gbeyîlataa performance the *posîa* missed the
singer's pause cue. The chorus, however, had heard
the cue and stopped. After the entire ensemble
had stopped, the *posîa* belatedly blew his whistle.
At this point, the vocal soloist commented:

> *Posîa nyan néi fé nia ni mèi káa ni?*
> Has the *posîa* forgotten to watch? (ATR453-55)

Token Gifts as Audience Response

   Once the pause is achieved, speeches are made
which frequently accompany token gifts to the performers from audience members. The speeches employ
exaggeration and allusion in order to enhance the
proferred token. Event participants judge and

evaluate the speaker's verbal skill.

This gift segment usually involves the identification of the giver, thanks to performers, or description of the token through exaggeration. One such speech, using the first two elements, praised a horn ensemble:

Kaa durii fêe, ka seyê, ka mãma.
You blowing the horns, thank you, thank you.

Nãa 6a Gãmai.
My name is Gamai.

Ŋã kula Gbonotaa.
I come from Gbonotaa.

Ŋa surôŋ lãa 6a kekula-polo.
My husband's name is Kekula-polo.

So kã seyê kpo kaa a dãmaa,
So thank you very much,

Fîlei dei gbinii ŋî su.
In this Friday evening (ATR416.5)

The token's value is not nearly as important as the style and flair of the speech. In the comment below, Saki had ended his praise speech and was handing the performers two cents as he said,

...ge ŋî dãla ono feere kã tî.
...then here are two hundred dollars (ATR416.6)

During the *maa-yêe* phase, the tokens given by the audience are an important impetus or deterrent to the continuation of the performance. If audience response is positive and tokens come frequently, the performers feel compelled to put forth ever better efforts. If the audience is unenthusiastic, the performance is likely to stop or not reach further heights of synchronization. Audience response is a very vital part of the total event. Performers relate stories of especially responsive, or cold, audiences they have had, gifts given, and speeches made.

The audience uses these pauses both to express thanks verbally, and to insert spoken *sãŋ* into the performance. That is, they respond to the performance of *sãŋ* with more *sãŋ*. The participants

in turn evaluate the quality of these speeches.
These speeches are not unique to the Kpelle, for
Hugo Zemp relates similar features in Dan per-
formance (1971:204-205).

At a more specific level, token gifts are
offered directly to certain dancers or performers
rather than to the *posîa* for the entire group. In
this case, no pause in the music sound occurs.
Rather, as the musician reaches a segmentation
point, the audience member steps forward and
hands the performer a coin. It is accepted without comment as the background music continues.
This is particularly common as a response to fine
dancing.

Ɖà Tee (Cutting-the-Edge)

During the *ɖà tee* (cutting-the-edge) phase of an
event, musical communication in the form of markers
moves the participants from the finite sphere of
performance back to everyday reality.[4] *Ɖà tee* cues
also move participants to the end of a song segment
or dance movement. *Ɖà tee* can thus occur at various levels of specificity, but in all cases it
implies the ending or delineation of an interaction.

The cutting-the-edge cue has some similarities
to that used for pauses. It is indicated by the
melodic descent, "pulling," and the syllable "èe."
Yet this cue indicates a more definitive break than
the pause cue. Figures 12 and 13, both performed
by the Noni group, are examples of this type of
cue. In Figure 12, the song end is cued by the
vocal soloist "pulling" on two levels. It occurs
in measure five as Moses Noni extends the last
word. It also occurs through foreshadowing on a
less specific level as the soloist repeats his
phrase a number of times prior to measure five and
does not introduce new material. The chorus,
then, needs but a simple cue to end: a "pulling"
of the last word of the phrase in measure five
(marked by a double asterisk). The song ends in
the measure immediately following.

Figure 12.   Cutting-the-Edge Cue
(ATR452.2/T34-36)

I am the False-rain,
Where I rise I do not fall.
False-rain doesn't fall there,
I am the False-rain,
Where I rise I do not fall.
False rain doesn't fall there.
I am the False rain,
Where I rise I do not fall.

Figure 13 is a similar example; the soloist "pulls" the phrase in measure seven as he slows down slightly. He also uses a descending vocal glide on the last note in measure seven to add further emphasis (marked by a double asterisk). The song ends in the next measure.

Figure 13. Cutting-the-Edge Cue
(ATR452.3/T32-39)

Sickness
Is on the child.

A music event ending is similar to a song ending, since events are made up of relatively parallel song segments. Certain unique devices, however, typify the closing of an event. A group
receives a *páma-seu*, a leave-taking token, upon
completing its obligation to the patron. Offering
this token is an important marker to the end of
the event, for it means that the interaction has
been satisfactorily achieved. The award of *páma-
seu* may be foreshadowed, for the performers may
indicate in song text that they are tired or are
approaching what they feel should be the end of
the event. Cues indicating this include,

Volôi ká lî-oo.
The sun is going, oh (ATR417.5)

or

Nua da lêe meni ma, ģoo a wêe pú-oo.
My people have stayed with the matter,
    my voice left yesterday.

Kâ lee mâ, ḿvii aâ kpɛɛ-ee.
You've stayed with me, I'm tired (ATR417.4).

A female vocalist used the following phrase to
tell the *kôɲkoma* (large plucked idiophone) player
that she was about to end the song;

Kôɲkoma, íwoo têe mâ.
Kóɲkoma, cut your voice from me (ATR438.2).

Moses Ŋoni often sang the following phrase before
ending an event:

Moses Ŋoni a ӿwelii e koôɲ-oo-we.
Moses Ŋoni wants to fly.

Ŋâ kê ɳá koôɲ, kpolo tâmaa kâa ḿberei.
If I want to fly, many shrubs are in my way (VTR704.1).

He also used a kinesic cue to communicate the
approaching end of a song. With a nod of the head,
he indicated that when the verse ended, the song
would end.
    In dance, a specific movement, also called *ɳá
tee*, signaled the segment's end. In discussing a
particular dancer's delay in giving this cut-off
cue, Moses Ŋoni said, "Gâ níi gooi" (It's still in
the feet).

Event Segmentation

    Structural segmentation in Kpelle events is an
important concept and music events show varying
degrees of segmentation. On one hand, segmentation is highly valued in the performance of entertainment music but, on the other hand, it is obscured in certain respects in the performance of
ritual and religious music. While entertainment
events, for example, emphasize segmented dance
movements, in the quasi-ritual *koli-gôɲ-sôɲ-pele*,
these segments are deliberately obscured.[5] This is
somewhat analogous to the contrast in segmentation
between *meni-pêle (chante fable)* and *woi-mêni-pele*
(epic). The *chante fable* is a self-contained,
single episode, dramatized musical folktale per-

formance.   But the epic is multi-episodic and the
storyteller obscures the segmentation of episodes
as he intermingles themes and characters from one
episode to another and introduces the upcoming
episode before he ends the present episode. More-
over, the storyteller never repeats an episode in
a single evening, for to do so would indicate he
had reached the end of his repertoire. No over-
all linear time progression connects the episodes,
the sequence of events occurring only *within* episodes. This further obliterates the Kpelle consideration of linear time passage.

PROCESS AND STRATEGY IN COMMUNICATING

Participants in Kpelle music performance manipulate cues and markers to coordinate and synchronize action. Through such communication and interaction processes, they emphasize two strategies:
communication according to hierarchical organization of the event participants; and communication
in an indirect manner. The hierarchy of music
event participants is characterized by a complex
system of part-counterpart roles interdependently
related to one another. That is, while individuals
have certain privileges in manipulating *sân*, the
"star" performer is always counter-balanced by a
counterpart with similar but less prominent status.
Soloists--vocal and instrumental--are the most
likely to initiate and manipulate cues and markers
in the process of creating an event. Their roles,
however, are not exclusive, for even as the Kpelle
performance emphasizes hierarchical communication
roles, the counterparts, to some extent, provide
balance.

The master drummer may evaluate what other performers are playing and prescribe a solution when
the music is not performed properly. The *fêli*
(goblet drum) player in both the Gbeyîlataa and
Noni groups use the following cue (Figure 14) to
the *gbùŋ-gbùŋ* (two-headed cylindrical drum) player
when the master drummer wants the *gbùŋ-gbùŋ* player
to speed up his tempo.

Figure 14.   Master Drummer Cuing the Gbùn-gbùn
(ATR429.3)

Gbùn-gbùn push it, Gbùn-gbùn push it,
Push it gbùn-gbùn.

A vocal soloist, as well as a master drummer, may
initiate a message concerning the quality of performance:

Ŋa ŋwêli di fáai zoo.
I want their responding to mesh (ATR414.3).

or

Wule zoo.
Mesh the song (ATR434.1).

or

Ka yée ke ŋulei ma, kwàla-pelee.
Keep your hands on the song, young initiates (ATR458.2/
T276).

In other situations, the vocal soloist expresses
appreciation of the choral performance by singing:

Kwàla ka seyè ka máma, Boo-wee.
Initiates thank you, thank you, Boo-wee.

Ka seyè ka máma kwàla-mu-na.
Thank you, thank you, initiates.

Nîai da zeu ke a nelee-ee-aa.
They are doing the thing well (ATR458.2/T276).

When the Gbeyîlataa master drummer is not
pleased with the group's performance, he plays a
curse employed out of the musical context as well.

Figure 15.   Master Drummer Cuing Group
(ATR429.4)

All, all of you have excrement on the buttocks.

A vocal soloist, in another instance, may sing
about the general ensemble performance.

Posîa wee, uule wôoi fê ni pîlau-nii-oo.
Posîa, the song voice has not yet gotten down (ATR458.3/
T287).

Not everyone has equal opportunity to manipulate
communication. While the soloists and *posîa* are
primary initiators in this activity, at certain
points, such as pauses, the audience has a prime
opportunity to become involved. Thus, the hierarchy changes during various phases of the event.
Cues and markers are ideally communicated in an
indirect manner. That is, participants interact
with one another through intermediaries as well as
through elusive verbal and musical images. When a
vocal soloist wants the ensemble to pause, she
uses *sâu* to communicate to the *posîa* who then com-
municates to the entire group. She is not doing
this to make herself understood. Such redundancy
is unnecessary to understanding, but it is status
enhancing and aesthetically pleasing. In this
situation, *sâu* as a quality of performance is
created when cues with obscure meanings are relayed through layers of individuals. The obscure

language and redundant cues and markers contribute
to a "thick" or "resonant" performance built up
through this complex interrelation and interaction.

   This complex interrelation develops processually.
Let us return to the example of a pause cue given
earlier in Figure 11. We can see that the layering
of cues as presented in the illustration did not
happen the first time this pause sequence occurred,
but if we consider a twelve-minute segment of the
event, eight pause cues are found. The cuing
sequence indicated in Figure 11 actually occurred
for pause segments 6, 7, and 8 only. The cues
for the first five pause segments are shown below:

Figure 16.   Process in Pause Cuing
                (ATR414)

Pause 1:

Pause 2:

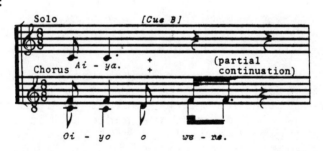

Pause 3:

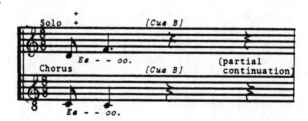

Pause 4:   Same as Pause 3 except with whistle added.

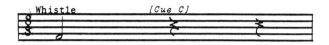

Pause 5:   Cue A, but Cue C does not follow and per-
           formance breaks down.

(complete
pause)

In pause sequence 5, the ensemble breaks down
completely when the *posîa* fails to respond to the
vocal soloist's cue. Figure 17 presents a flow
chart of all eight pause segments, each of which
becomes more elaborate as the performance pro-
ceeds. A variety of combinations is possible in
the layering of cues, but only when Cue C occurs
(blowing of whistle) does a complete pause ensue
In the other instances a partial continuation of
the performance occurs.

Figure 17.   Flow Chart of Eight Pause
              Cue Segments*

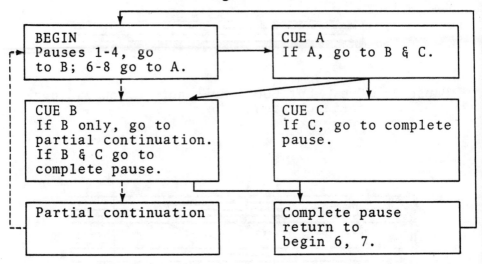

BEGIN Pauses 1-4, go to B; 6-8 go to A.	CUE A If A, go to B & C.
CUE B If B only, go to partial continuation. If B & C go to complete pause.	CUE C If C, go to complete pause.
Partial continuation	Complete pause return to begin 6, 7.

*Pause sequence 5 has been omitted because B
occurs but not C and the performance breaks down.

CONCLUSION

The communication in music events achieved
through markers and cues can be considered not only
for the audio channel, but for the kinesthetic-
visual, and other channels as well. Sound is primary in most instances, for the Kpelle stress this
communication channel both within the finite province of performance and in everyday life. But at
different times a cue or marker in some other channel may dominate communication. Further, the cue or
marker may be given in more than one channel at a
time, occurring simultaneously or sequentially.
    Cuing and marking are, at one level, necessary
in order to sustain an event. But at another level
these communication devices become part of the
aesthetic experience as they are multiplied and
created for the pleasure they bring to the event
participants. Cuing and marking were important for
both the Ŋoni and Gbeyîlataa performances. But the
indirect execution of cues and markers involving a
manipulation of hierarchy was more characteristic
of the Gbeyîlataa group, for the Ŋoni group relied
more on pre-arranged cues given directly to people
with more permanently fixed status and identity.

6

Significance and Meaning
in Events

Nale-seu wóo nĕe, di zeleu.
The voice of the struck things is sweet,
  hang them.

                              --Moses Noni, singer

This study began with a presentation of the disparate assumptions that ethnomusicologists, operating from different perspectives, have made concerning study object, context, analytic level, and
research framework. It then outlined a broad
theoretical perspective that was more unitary in
approach than either of the two main perspectives.
This involved choosing the music event, rather
than the song or music system, as the focal study
object; this object lies at an analytic level different from that of the other two main perspectives.
The use of music event as a study object has
conceptual validity from the Kpelle perspective.
For the Kpelle, music sound is conceptualized as
part of an integrally related cluster of dance,
speech, and kinesic-proxemic behavior. By focusing
on event, the researcher is able to look at these
clusters in relation to one another. There remains, however, the inescapable problem that the
present study of event still relies on analytic
techniques derived from both streams of ethnomusicology: musicology and anthropology. Therefore, it is not yet possible to achieve the ideal
unitary analysis nor to use analytic techniques
exclusively derived from the project's theoretical
requirements.
Furthermore, we cannot assume that the study of
the event encompasses all of the human activity
that is related and important to the understanding
of music. The event is necessarily only a starting

point for exploration of music systems. Despite
these problems, the present study yielded some
basic discoveries about how the Kpelle conceive of
music events.

Conclusion 1: *Audio communication is a primary
means of interaction both in everyday life and in
music events.* Not only is audio communication
highly valued, but other kinds of human experience
often are translated into sound terms for expres-
sive purposes. While visual aspects are part of a
performance, the sound remains dominant. An extension of this focus is the high value placed on
speech within Kpelle interaction. Furthermore,
timbre as descriptive of sound quality, is a very
important part of the total sound dimension, and
is noted and described to a great extent.

Conclusion 2: *Participants relate to one another in hierarchical, interdependent ways with
a shifting part-counterpart relationship typical
of the event interaction.* The part-counterpart
relationship is more than a simple hierarchical
arrangement, for it involves an interesting supporting role as a balance to the soloist's role.
Throughout the event the relationships shift and
alter to some extent.

Conclusion 3: *Music events are constructed of
interaction typified by sàu, a multi-faceted quality of dance, music, and speech exemplifying knowledge and aesthetically pleasing manipulation of
that knowledge.* *Sàu* expresses the faceting of
something and the exposition of that faceting in a
pleasing way. This is what the Kpelle consider
music to be--turning over sound, action, and object, individually or simultaneously to reveal a
new and yet unexposed part. The denser a performance is with *sàu*, the more pleasing it is considered to be.

Conclusion 4: *Entertainment events ideally involve a maximum number of participants--physically
present and surrogate--performing as many different parts as possible within the requirement of
maintaining a coherent whole.* The ideal structure
of Kpelle performance is created through the hocket technique in which the melody is constructed
of one- or two-note motifs contributed by different
performers. As the motifs interlock, the unity of
the melody is created.

Conclusion 5: *The temporal conceptualization of music events centers on expandable moments that are considered to have a three-dimensional spatial quality.* According to Kpelle thinking, the linear aspect of time is obscured, though not totally lost. Rather, within such moments, ideas, events, and people of many locales and times are incorporated into the music event.

Conclusion 6: *Entertainment events are segmented into numerous parts that come together through synchronization of performers' actions.* Dance movements, music sound, and speech are all ideally segmented in performance and then combined into a unitary whole. This segmentation of structure relates to Conclusion 4, involving the maximum number of participants performing many different parts.

Conclusion 7: *Cues and markers proliferate at nodal points in performance where maximum negotiation of structure and synchronization are required.* As a performance begins, ends, or reaches a new phase, cues and markers become an especially important way of synchronizing behavior.

MUSIC EVENTS AND CULTURE

Ethnomusicologists of various persuasions have been tantalized by the possible connections between music sound and other aspects of culture. The issue of meaning, however, as derived from the music-culture connection has not been examined comprehensively. Scholars either doubt that such connection exists or wonder why they have not found elegant examples. They search for symbolic meaning in a rhythmic pattern or melodic motif without stepping back to approach the question of meaning more broadly. Furthermore, the approach requires one not only to understand meanings, but meanings significant for a particular group of people.

At the most general level, we can explore the connections between music events and other culture systems by focusing on systems built up by the complex fitting together of human actions spanning space and time. We shift from the focus on isolated events and their participants. The generalizations are based on the empiric data obtained at the event level in participant-observation and interviews.

Considering the interaction observed in Kpelle music events, the music-culture connection can be stated from a different point of view. In music events, participants highlight elements of culture: focusing on them, turning them, and examining them. They point up certain features, consciously manipulating them. Therefore, some aspects of culture are more connected to music than others. It is not simply that some of these aspects are reflected, and others are not reflected. Rather they are subtly manipulated and toyed with in the context of musical interaction.

Certain major connections recur continually in Kpelle music events. The importance of the music-speech link is difficult to overstate. In Kpelle life, speaking is a highly valued skill. In music performance, by extension, the singer's skill in structuring the text is highly admired. When Kpelle informants were asked to comment on the qualities they considered important in a singer, they frequently ranked a singer who can sing fine texts equal to, or slightly better than a singer with a fine voice. Some said that a singer did not have a fine voice unless she or he was skillful in text construction.

In Kpelle, a language with three phonemic pitch levels, an intimate connection exists between speech and musical pitches, though one cannot assume a one-to-one correspondence. Furthermore, the master drummer and other performers represent rhythmic patterns with verbal mnemonic patterns. The rhythmic aspects of speech reflect the music's rhythm, and the pattern's vowels reflect the relative music pitch and timbre. Finally, speech metaphors describe musical actions. For example, one might say, "Mãla è mò," (The dance he spoke).

Social structure is connected with music performance, although the social structure of performance is different from that of everyday life. The personification of instruments and instrument parts, such as strings, reflects social structure, as does the manipulation of social relations within events. This manipulation not only involves the instruments, but the participants and their multiple identities. Certain social relations and interactions which are normally constrained are made permissible and even encouraged in music interaction. Solo singers can assume the role of a chief's critic when, in other situations, the

chief's actions would not be questioned. Within
the performance context, a musician interacts from
a high social position, although it is only held
within the finite sphere of performance. Performers also have license to criticize people and in-
stitutions not legitimately questioned within the
context of everyday interaction.

The music event interaction also incorporates
the presence and influence of surrogate participants to a much greater degree than in everyday
life. The more the performance incorporates ritual
and religious aspects, the more likely it is to
involve surrogate participants in the form of
spirits and predecessors. These personages must be
considered as an important aspect of the total
social structure, and their incorporation into
music events is of interest to the ethnomusicologist.

Music events related to the religious system
involve ritual activities of the Poro and Sande,
secret societies to which all adult Kpelle belong.
While music events occur in conjunction with these
activities, references to the Poro and Sande are
ubiquitous within entertainment events.[1]

Music is also associated with the special religious (sâle) societies, and each society, as
noted earlier, is marked by certain instrument combinations and characteristic music making. The
spirits may use the music context for communicating
with people, performing as surrogate participants.

Certain elements of the ritual-religious complex
apparently lack connection to music performance.
The numbers three for women, and four for men, are
significant in many life cycle activities. A new-
born girl is brought out for public viewing three
days after birth; a boy four days after birth.
The Sande secret society session lasts for three
years, the Poro four years. The death feast is
held three days after burial for a woman and four
days after burial for a man. Yet no evidence indicates that this quantitative focus carries over
into the music structure.

Music also relates to the subsistence system.
Nearly all Kpelle practice slash-and-burn
agriculture, and all the Gbeyîlataa musicians were
farmers, although none of the Noni group were so
engaged. Yet both were involved with the subsistence system, since it affects performance sched-
uling. That is, few music performances take place

during times of heavy farm work, but many music
performances occur during light work periods. In
the Central Kpelle area, for example, the rice
harvest season is finished in December. With the
conjunction of the Christmas and New Year's holi-
days and an abundance of food and cash, performance events cluster together. During the December to January period in 1975-76, entertainment
events for which the Gbeyîlataa and Noni groups
performed were numerous. The Gbeyîlataa group performed in their own town for a high feast staged
by the chief as well as for people in neighboring
town celebrations. Also during this season, a
number of parents presented their girls for initiation into the Sande society, coinciding with a time
when abundance could make it possible to pay performers and provide requisite gifts for the girls'
entry.

Music is crucial to Kpelle work cooperatives
which are especially strong in a town such as
Gbeyîlataa, although totally absent from the rubber
camp of the Nonis. In an activity such as bush-
clearing, the music is structured primarily in
hocket; this highly valued music structure in which
many people share responsibility for portions of
the melody coincides with a form of labor in which
the workers pool their energy in the most important
and crucial work of their lives.[2]

Music events are also connected with historical
changes in the political system. In the late
eighteenth and early nineteenth centuries, political rulers often supported court musicians, an act
which enhanced a ruler's status. But often these
musicians were also subtle critics within the
chiefdom, communicating in song and allusion that
which could not be spoken in ordinary speech. War
chiefs, *kó-kaloŋ,* also supported musicians who accompanied them into battle, and who were purport-
edly exempt from capture if they immediately de-
clared their allegiance to the winning chief when
their own chief was defeated.

In Gbeyîlataa, the town's founder retained several court musicians until the 1930's. He employed
a harp-lute (*keráŋ-noŋ-koniŋ*) player, who had been
brought from the northern Kpelle area, in addition
to a flute and drum ensemble. During the present
study, court musicians were rare in the Kpelle area
and non-existent in Gbeyîlataa. But the *pêle-kaloŋ*
today remains a direct link to the political sys-

tem. The Gbeyîlataa and Noni group performances
reflected elements of the Liberian national government, including, for example, comments on current
political events of national scope. Furthermore,
the Gbeyîlataa group, when using *sôya* (soldiers) to
control performers, reflected a model learned from
the national government. The activities of the
Gbeyîlataa treasurer who kept the group's funds were
also based on a Western model, as were more of the
posîa who incorporated the roles of a policeman
and master of ceremonies.

SIGNIFICANCE OF MUSIC EVENTS
AS CULTURAL PERFORMANCES

While broad connections exist between the music
system and other cultural systems, it is also
possible to focus even more narrowly on events and
their cultural significance.

Assigning significance for any single event is
not a simple matter, and the present study suggests
that the event's significance varies depending upon
the participant's perspective. For example, if we
consider a typical performance at a death feast,
the multiple aspects of significance exist. When
Neeto staged a feast after the death of his mother,
he hired musicians from another community to play
entertainment music such as might be found at any
entertainment event, rather than the traditional
funeral dirges. A number of the audience had little acquaintance with the bereaved family, and
simply came to enjoy the music. For them, the
event's significance was primarily entertainment.
For the family and a few close friends, the significance was primarily release from sadness--the
proper activity to commemorate the passing of a
loved one to the world of the spirits and ancestors. For the musicians, the event's significance
related to the praise and limited financial com-
pensation they received in a community with which
they had varying degrees of social relationship.[3]
The music performances of the Noni group are
significant as cultural performances because the
performers interpret and manipulate Western ideas
in interactions that represent an interface of
Kpelle and Western culture. The group highlights
ambiguity between Kpelle and Western culture, ex-
hibiting fundamentally Kpelle aspects while over-

laying and manipulating their understanding of
Western notions. This makes the Nonis acceptable
and even admired as performers by a great number
of people. Yet the reasons people give for their
admiration vary widely. To the young people, the
Nonis appear avant-garde Western pop, while at the
same time they are considered purveyors of a new
style of Kpelle music still retaining respectable
traditional elements.

The Nonis seek to incorporate the creation of
sâu, that most valued aspect of Kpelle tradition,
into their music. But they also make Western
music elements--linear and self-centered texts,
verse form, extended and unison choral response,
fixed accompaniment parts--understandable and
acceptable to many Kpelle people. The duality of
this is illustrated by one song title, alternately
understood, in English, as "Alleluia," or, in
Kpelle, as "A lí lón yai" (He is going to buy a
child). In the context of sung performance one
can easily hear either alternative, given the
elisions that occur. Similar song title manipulation could either be "Sanno," or "Sân non." The
former is a name found in coastal language; the
latter is Kpelle for "proverb child."

The Gbeyîlataa group also exhibits and manipulates Western cultural ideas in their performances.
But their music structure does not contain the
basic Western aspects present in the Noni performance, most particularly, textual linearity and
nearly tempered scale structures. Western elements
are additions to basic Kpelle construction.[4]

In the Kpelle case, music offers people unique
opportunities to manipulate aspects of culture, for
music, relying to a great extent on the audio
medium, allows the manipulating and structuring of
interaction in multiple dimensions of time. Within a relatively short duration of clock time, a
very dense, complex interaction situation is possible, incorporating entities from the spirit and
ancestor worlds. No other interaction situation
incorporates as many individuals--physically present as well as surrogate--into a linkage of action
in such a short space of time. And what an ethnomusicologist measures as time length, the Kpelle
describe as the density of a moment. In Kpelle
aesthetic terms, this is the medium *par excellence*
for achieving multiple dimensions of interaction
among individuals.

The complexity of achieving some level of synchronous interaction was evident during the field observations. Multiple negotiations had to succeed before a performance occurred. And for the ethnomusicologist, the hours preceding an event were initially difficult to understand. Disconnected interactions appeared to be taking place in various locations around the town, the direction of which were difficult to ascertain. Yet when the negotiations succeeded, the unity of interaction that produced music sound contrasted sharply to the multiple directions of prior interactions. The focus performance brought to interaction was astounding. Even after observing this process many times, I still viewed it with amazement and appreciation for the intricacies of linking human behavior which it revealed.

Furthermore, the interaction that characterizes Kpelle performance is not mass unison. Rather it is a shifting hierarchy of individual expression against a background of unison support. In the music event, people can interact with individuals in specific ways not possible or appropriate in everyday life. They express the strong emotion they may experience in their lives. If they are happy, performance multiplies their happiness as it gives voice to that feeling. If they are sad, performance offers them a chance to forget their sadness.

Music performance represents a cultural microcosm. But it is more than a presentation of culture on a miniature scale. Rather, it is an occasion for the confirmation or restructuring of relationships within a separate but related sphere of interaction. It is a sphere rich in ideas not only of the here and now, but of other places and times. This provides a sumptuous context in which manipulation of the elements can occur. The quality of *sâŋ* that appears occasionally in everyday interaction becomes the very pivot and center of music performance.

Music events are significant in that they are uniquely created by the selection and manipulation of the multiple facets of everyday life. In the creation of a performance, participants manipulate things which both reflect culture and are culture, but are not the same as everyday life. This minute turning of experience to expose and juxtapose aspects in time creates the "thick performance"

that is different from everyday life. It is part
of *pêle*, that finite sphere of which music is a
part.

Music, then both reflects and restructures the
culture, and can be understood as we can understand
nuance, subtlety, and ambiguity in the creation of
audio phenomena. For the Kpelle, music is most
crucially centered in these features, and these
areas are revealed only to those with a firm
understanding and grounding in the basic cultural
system of Kpelle life.

IMPLICATIONS OF CONCLUSIONS

The conclusions demonstrate the interconnected-
ness of the sound and behavior aspects of performance. The Kpelle consider the sounds themselves
to be personified voices, and conceive of the
sounds as combining in terms of social interaction,
which reflects features of the social structure.

The connections between the culture and the
performance, however, are not simply mutual reflec-
tions of similar entities. Rather, within the
event we can observe special manipulations of
social relations as the music is created, and
therefore, the event is more than a simple reflection of something else: it is a processual creation
within a finite sphere of reality.

The Kpelle conception emphasizes the facetedness
of performance and combination in a three-dimen-
sionally oriented event. While the hocketing technique has been identified in previous studies of
African music, it has not been defined according
to an indigenous conceptualization, nor have the
connections to social structure and interaction
been incorporated into the analysis. The Kpelle
segmentation of musical structure and related ideas
involves more than sound. In relation to ritual,
for example, the implications are more evident if
one looks holistically at musical interaction at
various analytic levels.

While ethnomusicologists in the past have
pointed out that staff notation is inadequate for
transcribing African music in which pitches are
not of the tempered octave, it becomes evident
that the linear time conception of staff notation
is an equally crucial problem. The Western notation system lacks the flexibility crucial to re-

presenting music in the way the Kpelle conceive it. It is important that this problem be given serious consideration in further attempts to improve techniques.

The present study shows that cuing and marking are communication devices which are not only useful for achieving synchronization but are also essential for the aesthetic aspects of Kpelle performance. They become most prominent during performance phases when the negotiation of meaning becomes most problematic. If studied processually in context, these devices are found to be not static, but changing and developing aspects dependent upon the many factors of the total music event.

This study points to the dynamic aspect of performance and does not assume that music is only a structural object. The Kpelle, who deemphasize the linear aspect of time, nevertheless emphasize the processual, dynamic nature of musical interaction within the expandable moments of performance. Furthermore, the Kpelle study shows how essential negotiation is for creating a performance event. For the Kpelle, music events are not preformed, but rather are dynamic creations built of choices made by performers as they interact and communicate with other event participants.

The theoretical framework, as well as the methods and techniques employed, were crucial to the conclusions drawn. The use of sensitizing concepts allowed for the discovery of the Kpelle conceptions of musical structure. The feedback interviews facilitated participants' explication of ideas and aspects of Kpelle performance that had not been considered in previous interview research. These techniques generated enormous amounts of data, the value of which is clear. What is needed now is comparative data provided by more research in other cultures. With such research, the broad generalizations that should charactertize ethnomusicology will be possible, undergirded by the rich data yielded by such techniques. Studies in ethnomusicology will exhibit both the valued detail of musicology and the valued generalization of anthropology in a more unitary approach to research.

Appendix A

Performance by Gbeyîlataa group, VTR705.
Participants in interview: Male chorus members Zõo
(Z) and Seŋkpe (S); researcher (R).
Date of interview: 21 April 1976.

TEXT

Z: *Kpolâŋ kpolâŋ kâ tî.*[1]
That's *kpolâŋ kpolâŋ.*

Seka-sokokpâ.

Tǎi da 6a pâi kei mǎlai, 6a ke pâi mǎla ʉâ tee,
Sometimes when you are coming to dance, when you are
    coming to cut the dance off,

ī ke îkoo tê gie pôlu.
you raise your feet behind one another.

Sokokpâ kâ tî.
That's *sokokpâ.*

Nyîni ...kpolâŋ kpolâŋ kâ tî.
That...that's *kpolâŋ kpolâŋ.*

Ba ke mǎlai, mǎla zâŋ kâ tî 6a ke gulâi ma.
When you are dancing, those are the dance *sâŋ* you are
    taking off of it.[2]

Zâŋ-ŋai kâ tî da ke gulâi ma.
Those are the *sâŋ* they are taking off of it.

Mm. Sokokpâ kâ tî.
Mm. That's *sokokpâ.*

138

A ke pâi mǎla kôo pîlan -nii, nyà 6ê a ke gêi foi.
When he's going to begin dancing, that's what he does
first.

R: *Gáa zu kpêi?*
Is he clearing the inside?

Z: *Owei.*
Yes.

Gê mǎlai zu kpê.
He's clearing the inside of the dance.

Í gôlon, nyîni, 6a ke pâi mǎn kei, 6a ke mǎlai,
You know, this, when you are coming to do it, when you
are dancing,

6a lee mǎlai, î kê îkoo kee nî.
you keep dancing, you do your feet thus.

Í kê vêli-yale-nuu su kôon kɔon.
You are testing, testing the master drummer.

A ke pori fêli yalêi, i gôlon ma.
If he can play the *fêli*, you will know by it.[3]

Nyà ká tî a ke gêi tî lai...
And so he is doing that...

A ke mǎlai tî...nalôn a lee nô vêlii yalêi tî,
When he's dancing thus...the man keeps playing the
fêli thus,

ê nôno mǎlai pêne nâ.
then he turns the dance on edge.

Ge bene nâ, ge ge nô tî, a gêe nalôn tî a fêli yale
He turns it on edge, doing thus in order to test

ge zu kɔon.
the drummer.

...Sokokpâ ká tî. Mn. Ba gâai?
...That's *sokokpâ*. Yes. Do you see?

A ke sokokpâ têei, Nyai-lá fa pɔri vêlii yalêi.
When he's cutting *sokokpâ*, Nyai-lá can't play the *fêli*.

So nya ká tî è ǹyêei ke ɯí ma.
So that's why he did his hand this way to him.

Nɏee ma, "Îfe pori ma."
He said to him, "You can't do it."

Sokokpâ nô kpô nô ká tî a dêei tî.
That's just *sokokpâ* he's cutting.

Kpolâɯ kpolâɯ ká tî.
That's *kpolâɯ kpolâɯ.*

...Í gôloɯ, vê pori fêli ma.
...You know, he isn't accomplished on the *fêli.*

Da kpera a gîe.
They stop together.

A maa kôri ma.
He's learning it.

Mǎlai 6a ke pâi mǎlai 6erei 6e 6a ke mǎlai la...
When you are going to dance, that is how you dance...

Kpâɯ kpâɯ ká tî.
That's *kpâɯ kpâɯ.*

I gôloɯ, 6a ke mǎlai. Ba ke mǎlai tî, nuui ge vêlii yale,
You know, you are dancing. When you are dancing thus, the

   ge vêlii yale kpâɯ kpâɯ.
   person is playing the *fêli kpâɯ kpâɯ.*

Mɱ̃. *Ba gâai. Ge lono fêli ma.*
Mm. You see. He is talking on the *fêli.*

Mɱ̃. *Wokpêe a pâ naa. A ke mǎlai, ge gbono tumo.*
Mm. Wokpêe has come there. As he dances, he shakes his
body.

Ge nyee-ɯá mâɯ ke.
He does thus with his hands.

Kpâɯ kpâɯ tono nô ká tî a niî mâɯ kêi tî.
The one *kpâɯ kpâɯ* is what he is doing.

Kpolâɯ kpolâɯ ká tî.
That's *kpolâɯ kpolâɯ.*

Sokokpâ kâ tî e ke dêei ke.
He was cutting *sokokpâ.*

E lee sokokpâ teei, ge nono kpolâu kpolâu tee nono.
He kept cutting *sokokpâ,* then he was cutting *kpolâu
    kpolâu.*

A ke vêli-yale-nuui su kôou nii.
He is testing the master drummer.

Ba lee sokokpâ têei, 6a nôno bene ñâ.
You keep cutting *sokokpâ,* and again turn it on edge.

So berei da kâa ge la.
So that's how they do it.

Kao kpîu bere 6ê da kâa ge la, ge fêli yale pere lê ma.
Even Kao did it that way when he was showing him how to
    play the *feli.*

Nuai di kê mãla, da ke mãlai, da ke bene, penei ge kô ma.
The people were dancing, and when they are dancing, they
    change it, change it and he tries it.

E lêe kôi ma, ê nâa pori fêli yale pere ma.
He kept trying until he is now accomplished at playing
    fêli.

...Mm. Ba gaai, die Nyai-la yêe maa tinauooi.
...Mm. Do you see, they say Nyai-la's hands are
    turned around.

Nyiui 6ê di ke mo.
This is what they were saying.

R: *Da ke die nuu yêe maa tînauooi, uo su-kûlai 6a lê?*
When they say a person's hands are turned around, what
    does it mean?

Z: *No su-kûlai 6a a ke vêlii yalêi, nuui a ke mãlai a maa
    felaa.*
Its meaning is that when he is playing the *fêli,* the per-
    son is dancing fast.

Nyau ñyêe maa tînauooi vêlii yalêi, nei uî ke mãla a
And his hands are turned around in playing the *fêli*

    maa felaa.
    while this person is dancing fast.

S: *Goo maa fêlaai e têe nuui yêe ma.*
His feet are faster than the person's hands.

Z: *Ba pâi kêi da su-kûlai mî.*
You will be explaining some for me.

Ba gâai, a ke mǎlai fie-fie. Ba gâai.
You see, he's dancing fast. You see.

Kpolân kpolân kâ tî a pa nâa dêei.
That's *kpolân kpolân* that he is now coming to cut.

Nuui fé pâi kpolân têei. A pa nâa toôi.
The person will not cut *kpolân*. He will stand.

...Î gôlon, 6a lee mǎlai, i6arâa-nuu a ke mǎlai a nǎna.
...You know, you keep dancing, your fellow is dancing
    hard.

Ba kpolân kpolân tee 6îan.
You are cutting *kpolân kpolân* yourself.

Î pâ î tôo bôo-nǎ, 6îan î kê mǎla.
You come and stand in his place and dance.

Berei 6ê da gêi lai, kâ ke kâ kîe ni maa fâlen nii.
That's how they do it, you change with each other.

Kpolân kpolân. Mm̂.

Fê mǎlai nyîni lâa kôlon oo.
I don't know the name of this dance.

A kê nô gêi gê zu-kôon.
He's just doing it and testing.

Ge vêli-yale-nuui su-kôon.
He's testing the master drummer.

Mm̂. Ba gâai.
Mm. You see.

Mǎla nyîni nuai di fê gôlon 6ê pere.
This dance, the people here don't know.

Mm̂. Dî fê gôlon. Î gôlon 6ê-pere ni 6ê e ke mǎlai la
Mm. They don't know it. Here is where he was dancing

a mǎla tí gofe su, kêlee nuai di fê pori ma fèli yalèi.
that dance in the coffee [farm], but the people couldn't
   play the *fèli* properly for it.

R: *Di zou lê meni ma?*
   Why did they catch him?   [The crowd restrains a dancer.]

Z: *Di zou.   Í gólou, di ke nâa vèli têe Nyai-lá po.*
   They caught him.   You know, they were giving the *fèli*
      to Nyai-lá.

   ...So dîe ma, too tí í 6oðoi.
   ...So they said to him, "Stop, you are stupid."

Wokpêe ka toði tí.
That's Wokpêe standing.

Kêe ka ke zu-kôou ni ka ke da 6o mî-ee.
Be testing some and saying some for me.   [spoken to some
   girls watching playback]

Kpolâu kpolâu kpô nô kâ tí a ke mǎlai.
That's *kpolâu kpolâu* he's dancing.

Ge kpolâu kpolâu tee.
He's cutting *kpolâu kpolâu.*

Kpanâ-lou kâ toði tí.
That's Kpanâ-lou standing there.

Ka ke meni-uâi uí su-kûlai mî ee.   Kâ kê da lê.
Explain some of these matters for me.   Show some.

Mǎla tônoi kpô nô kâ a gêi tí.
That's the same dance he's doing.

Kpolâu kpolâu kâ tí.
That's *kpolâu kpolâu.*

Due a pâ teêi naa.
Due is coming to pass there.

Kpolâu kpolâu

R: *Ŋo uâ tee 6a lê?*
   What is its cut off?

Z: *Í gôlon, 6a lee mǎlai, 6a ke pâi nǎ tee, í tôo.*
   You know, you keep dancing, and when you are going to cut
      it off, you stand.

   Mǎla-nuui da vêli-yale-nuui di nǎ tée kpô nô a gîe.
   The dancer and the master drummer cut it off together.

S: *Zoo 6ê tî?*
   Is that Zoo?

Z: *Mm̂.*

S: *Zoo-lon a mǎla nyan oo.*
   Zoo-lon can dance, oh.

R: *A nii zu kpêi?*
   Is he still clearing out the inside?

Z: *Mm̂. Sokokpâ kǎ tî.*
   Mm. That's *Sokokpâ.*

S: *Sokokpâ kǎ tî. Zoo-lon nyan a mǎla fe.*
   That's *sokokpâ.* Zoo-lon dances *fe.*

Z: *A mǎla a nǎna, nya 6ê da ke a mǎla fe*
   He dances hard, that's why they say he dances *fe.*

S: *Nooi è mǎla noii sǔ tono, oo. È mǎla kpô e mǎla kpô, oo.*
   The boy danced once in the land, oh. He danced, he really
      danced, oh.

   Lôkin kǎ tî.
   That's *lôkin.*

   Sokokpâ kǎ tî.
   That's *sokokpâ.*

   A pâi toôi 6ê. Da pâi kpulôn nii.
   He will stand here. They will fasten together.

   Tǎi nuui a pâi leei mǎlai, e kpulôn ma.
   When the person is going to keep dancing, he will fasten
      to him.

   Í 6arâa-nuui ê pâ ê kpulôn ya.
   Your fellow comes and fastens on to you.

   Ka nỳa kǎ nôno mǎla a gie, ka nǎ tee a gie.
   You and he dance together, you cut off together.

Nyan ê lí ê tôo.
Then he goes and stands.

...Nyee di fâa nulei mâ a nâ nâna.
...He says they should answer the song hard.

Kpân kpân kâ tí...a ke gêi tí.
That's *kpân kpân*...that he is doing.

Seka-sokokpâ kâ tí.
That's *seka-sokokpâ.*

S: *Sokokpâ kâ tí a ke nâ têei.*
That's *sokokpâ* that he's cutting off.

R: *A nâ têe len? Ge kula pòlu?*
How does he cut it off? Does he go back?

S: *Owei.*
Yes.

S: *Kpân kpân kâ tí e ke deêi tí, ge ní e kula pòlu.*
That's *kpân kpân* he was cutting, then he went back.

Z: *...Masakoitaa.*
[location of performance]

S: *Masakoitaa berei mâ kâ tí oo.*
That's on the road to Masakoitaa, oh.

Z: *Mm-mm. Bâlon wuri mû.*
Mm-mm. Under the plum tree.

S: *Oo.*
Oh.

Z: *Kèlen kêlen kâ à kè deêi tí nûu kê mâla tòno tôno.*
That's *kèlen, kêlen* as a person dances one, one.

Sokokpâ kâ tí.
That's *sokokpâ.*

...Nôo lêleei fe.
...His voice is fine *fe.*

R: *A nâ têe a nun tí?*
Does he cut it off with his head?

Z: *Mm. Nyee ve pori fèli yalèi.*
   Mm. He says [by moving his head] that he can't play the
   fèli.

S: *À kè a wala fèli yalèi a nun kpemen.*
   If he isn't playing the *fèli* he shakes his head.

Z: *A ná tee.*
   He cuts it off.

S: *Nyee, "Ka pá tèe na kâa."*
   He says, "Come pass."

   ...Lôkin ká a dèei tí. A ge tí nô gé sokokpâ tèei.
   ...That's *lôkin* that he's cutting. Then he cuts
   sokokpâ.

   Lôkin kpô nô ká tí.
   That's *lôkin.*

   Sokokpâ. Mm.

   Mălai nen ká tí a gbe naa.
   That's the tongue of the dance he's chasing from there.

S: *Nen. Nyíti í ge maa e nĕe.*
   Tongue. That which you do to make it sweet.

Z: *A gée maa é nĕe, gé măla.*
   In order for it to be sweet, he dances.

   Díe nooi a măla.
   They say the boy dances.

   A măla a nána.
   He dances hard.

   Maa lèn ná ká a ke gbèi. Ba doo pere kâa?
   He's chasing the edge of the tongue. Do you see his
   stance?

K: *Lôkin 6ê tí?*
   Is that *lôkin?*

S: *Owei.*
   Yes.

Núu a ke mǎlai, gê tuǎn tue pêre, a ke mǎlai ge pa pǒlu.
If a person is dancing he pushes forward, if he dances he
   comes back.

...So ąo mǎla pere kâ tí.
...So that's his way of dancing.

Sokokpâ...

Kpolâŋ kpolâŋ kâ a dêei tí.
That's kpolâŋ kpolâŋ he's cutting.

A ąôno kê lí a too.
He's again going to stand.

Mǎla kpô le ke, di fê kê ąí gêi a ꞥêlee oo.
The dance the other day, they weren't doing it well.

R: Lôkiŋ?

Z: Owei.
   Yes

   Sokokpâ kâ tí.
   That's sokokpâ.

   A pâi pêle kei saaɓa.
   He will play three times.

   Lôkiŋ kpô ąô kâ tí.
   That's just lôkiŋ.

   Kpolâŋ kpolâŋ kâ tí a deêi.
   That's kpolâŋ kpolâŋ he's cutting.

S: Keema fê pâ ni ee?
   Didn't Keema come?

Z: Mǎlai neą kâ tí a gbêi, a gêe a pôri mǎlai.
   That's the tongue of the dance he's chasing, that he can
      dance.

S: Oo Gbee-ąâ mǎlai kêtei.
   Oh Gbee-ąâ's dance is big.

Z: Gbee-ąâ fa pôri mǎlai.
   Gbee-ąâ can't dance.

Lôkin kpô nô kâ tí.
That's just *lôkin.*

S: *Lonîi kâ tí.   A mǎla mòoi.*
That's Lonîi.   He really dances.

Kpolǎn kpolǎn.

Sokokpâ kâ a dèei tí.
That's *sokokpâ* he's cutting

Nooi tí a mǎla kpô.
That boy really dances.

Mǎlai zu nen kpô kâ a gbèi tí.
The dance's inside tongue is what he is chasing.

...Sokokpâ kâ a dèei tí.
...That's *sokokpâ* that he is cutting.

Appendix B

Three Kpelle people watched the same videotape segment of a Koli-gón-són performance by the Gbey-îlataa group. Texts and translations of the feedback interviews follow. Event segment: VTR709.60-85 (2.5 minutes).

FEEDBACK INTERVIEW I

Source: ATR616.1
Participants in interview: Kpetê Dan (K), dancer in the group who was not present at the performance; researcher (R); Yakpalo (Y), research assistant.

TEXT

R: *Lê mǎla 6é a gèi tí?*
What dance is he doing?

K: *A goo teêi gîe pòlu.*
He's passing his feet behind each other.

R: *Nyîti...lê 6e?*
That...what is it?

K: *Nyîti, sólimo kâ gǎa mǎlai tí.*
That, that is *sólimo* he's dancing.

R: *Oôo.*

Y: *Lê sén?*
What thing?

149

K: *Sólimo.*

R: *Oðo.*

K: *Ee-êe.*
   [Yes.]

R: *Lê 6ê a ke pokɔn ni?*
   What is he imitating?

K: *Koli-gɔn-sɔn no kpawoi kâ tî?*
   That's *koli-gɔn-sɔn's* hook.

R: *No lê?*
   His what?

K: *No kpawo.*
   His hook.

R: *Oðo, kpawo.*
   Oh, hook.

K: *Ee. Zen tî da ke ma kêrere, kere î gôlon?*
   [Yes.] That thing they call *kêrere*, you know it don't
      you?

   Da gonâi saai la.
   They carve mortars with it.

   Nyà kâ tî.
   That is it.

R: *Lê 6ê a gêi tî, ge nyee pele?*
   What is he doing when he puts his hands down?

K: *Gaa zamai su têei naa.*
   He's cutting his middle [waist].

R: *Mãlai tî a sen ta pɔkon?*
   That dance, does it imitate something?

K: *Mm̃.*
   [Yes.]

R: *Nyà 6à lê?*
   What is it?

(Researcher stopped videotape recorder)

A ke mǎlai tǐ ke, lê 6ê a pokôu ni?
When he is doing that dance, what is he imitating?

K: *Yuu noo, seu da kǎ da kê ma sâu-salo.*
You know, there is something they call *sâu-salo.*

A woni stǐ da.
A type of bird.

R: *Lê?*
What?

K: *Nyà 6ê gaa bokôu ni.*
That is what he is imitating.

R: *A sâu-salo?*
San-salo?

K: *Mm̃-m̃m.*
[Yes.]

No berei a kê siâi la.   Berei...ma pôkou kǎ a gêi tǐ.
Its way of walking.   The way...the imitation he's doing.

R: *Ba pôri fâai ma Yakpalo?*
Can you agree to it Yakpalo?

Berêi sâu-salo a siâi la.
The way *sâu-salo* walks.

Y: *Mm̃.*   (Researcher starts VTR again.)
[Yes.]

K: *Yuu stǐ, naa a ke vǒolenii, tǎi da a gêe ê kolo kpêle.*
You see, it is ruffling its feathers, maybe to eat a worm.

Ma mǎlai kǎ a gêi tǐ. Ê.
That is the dance it is doing.

R: *Nyǐtǐ.*
That.

Ê. Mare-kêe kǎ uǐ.   (Researcher stops VTR.)
Eh. Here is a question.

K: *Mm̃.*
[Yes.]

R: *Núu da è kè mâ...nèei-ɲai dî ke 6ê nɔ̀kui tî su,*
   Someone told me...the women who were here last week,

    dî ke mâ, núu fa koli-gɔ́ɲ-sɔ́ɲ mǎla ɲǎ tee.
       they told me that a person does not cut off *koli-gɔ́ɲ-sɔ́ɲ* dance.

K: *Mm̃.   Di fa ɲǎ tee.*
   [Yes.] They don't cut off the edge.

R: *No su-kûlai 6a lé?*
   What is its meaning?

    Nuui a kula naa, ve pâi ɲǎ teei?
   When a person leaves there, he won't cut the edge?

K: *Eè.   A lee nó mǎlai...6a lee nó mǎlai...6a lee nó*
   Eh. He just keeps dancing...you just keep dancing

    mǎlai...tǎi da, da kpa gólou 6a tǔa naa,
   ...you just keep dancing, sometimes, when they know
      you've been there a long time,

    nuu da nyee é pǎ naa, 6îau î kula naa.
   a person says he will come there, you get out of there.

R: *Gе nî di fa ɲǎ tee lé meni ma?*
   Then why don't they cut it off?

K: *Eè-ée.   Yuu noo, ɲǎ tee fé ma.*
   [No.] You know, there is no edge cutting.

Nya 6a zǎu fa no ke ikôi.
That is, there is no longer *sǎu* in your stomach.

Nyîi 6a pɔ̀ri ɲǎ tee la.
That with which you can cut the edge.

Ba lee nó mǎlai kpô nô, 6a lee nó mǎlai kpô nô.
You just keep dancing, you just keep dancing.

Ba kpa tǎya ké, nyǎ 6ǎ îfii a kpa kpée,
When you get tired, that is, your breath is finished,

    î6arǎa nuui é pǎ naa.
   your fellow comes there.

R: *Berêi 6ê ka bêlei kpete la, a gêe di fe nâ tee?*
   Is that the way you arranged it, that they don't cut it
     off?

K: *Mîn. Fêe nô di ke wule da kpeni toôi.*
   [Yes.] Except they sing a different song.

   Kêe koli-gôn-sôn mãlai, kûmo kûa a gêe ku fa nâ tee.
   But *koli-gôn-sôn* dance, we said among ourselves that we
     don't cut the edge.

K: *Gêe nô yê bêlei nyti da kê ma gbɔ-pele.*
   It's just like the performance they call *gbɔ-pele.*

   Di fa gbɔ-pele nâ teêi.
   They don't cut off the edge of *gbɔ-pele.*

R: *Í bêlei ti kôlon?*
   Do you know that performance?

   Di fa nâ tee?
   They don't cut off the edge?

K: *Mîn-mîm.*
   [Yes.]

R: *Nô su-kûlai 6a lê?*
   What is its meaning?

   ...Ba kenemâ ke oo da kula naa fêe di nâ tee.
   ...If you do *kenemâ* or when they leave there they must
     cut off the edge.

   Da wala ge ti nûai da kê yêlei.
   If they don't do that, people laugh.

K: *Yuu noo, gâa zalei nɔ wooi ma.*
   You know, it is on the word of the medicine.

   Di fa bêlei nâ tee.
   They can't cut off the edge of the performance.

R: *Oo-ðo.*
   Oh.

   Ba lee nô gêi kpô nô, 6a lee nô gêi,
   You just keep doing it, you just keep doing it,

ḯfii a kpee, ḯ kula naa.
when your breath is finished, you get out of there.

Ba gàai, nèi tḯ mãlai a gèi tḯ, a pãi lee nó nãa,
You see that guy, the dance he's doing, he will just
   stay there,

vḯi a kpee ê kúla naa.
when his breath is finished, he will leave there.

R: *Oo-ðo.*
   Oh.

FEEDBACK INTERVIEW II

Source: ATR616.2
Participants in interview: Nyai-lá Saki Gbôn-pîlan
(N), master drummer for the event; researcher (R).

TEXT

N: *Pàwa-nuui kã tḯ koli-gón-són su.*
   That's the power person in *koli-gón-són.*

R: *Ee?*
   Huh?

N: *Mãla kã ã mòi tḯ.*
   That's the dance he's speaking.

   Pàwa-nuui kã tḯ.
   That's the power person.

   Nyà 6à pàwa mãlai kê.
   He's the one that does the power dance.

R: *No su-kùlai 6a lê?*
   What is its meaning?

N: *No su-kŭlai 6a, berêi nŭai da ké nala-woo 6ŏi lai,*
   Its meaning is, the way the people preach God's word,

      di ke kpetin kpetin, nya 6ê a ma mălai ké.
      they tremble, tremble, so it is he's doing that dance.

R: *Oo-ŏo.*
   Oh.

N: *Mm̂.*
   [Yes.]

R: *Lê 6ê a gêi tî? Nurîi tî găa nyêei...*
   What is he doing? The wood that is in his hand...

N: *Ee? Koli-gón-són wuri ta...kpawo kă tî.*
   Huh? *Koli-gón-són* wood...that's a hook.

   Gbawoi a zaa nŭai su, nya kă tî.
   The hook that he puts through people, that's it.

R: *A lê?*
   He what?

N: *Gbawoi a zaa nŭai su, nya kă tî.*
   The hook that he puts through people, that's it.

   Mm̂-m̂m. ...Păwa mălai kă a ke gêi tî.
   [Yes.] ...That's the power dance he is doing.

R: *Lê 6ê a gêi tî a nurîi tî ge bokôn?*
   What is he doing with that wood and imitating?

N: *Berêi a nurîi saa lai zăai su nya kă a bokôn kêi tî.*
   The way he pierces the wood into things, that's what he
      is imitating.

R: *Nyîti, ge pène péne tî.*
   That, he's turning, turning thus.

N: *Sekekpă nô kă a dêei tî.*
   He's just cutting *sekekpă* [dance step].

   Kee, nyini kêlee...gaa nô a măla. Mm̂.
   But, all this...is just dance. [Yes.]

FEEDBACK INTERVIEW III

Source: ATR616.3
Participants in interview: Zõo Wĩi (Z), dancer in
the event but not in this particular segment; researcher (R).

TEXT

Z: *Mole Fîlakaa kâ tî.*
That's Mole Fîlakaa.

R: *Le mǎla 6e a gêi tî?*
What dance is he doing?

Z: *Koli-gõn-sõn mǎla kâ tî.*
That's *koli-gõn-sõn* dance.

R: *Lê 6ê a bokõn ni?*
What is he imitating?

Nurîi tî nyêei, lê wuru 6ê nî?
That wood in his hand, what wood is it?

Z: *Nurîi tî ga nõ a...*
That wood is just...

Ba kpawo kâai? Gaa feere.
Do you see the hook? There are two.

Nuu a ke zon ni nî.
A person holds it thus.

Yuu sii, î ke mǎla la.
You see, you dance with it.

Nyiti kâa a mǎla sen, yuu sii.
That is a dance thing, you see.

R: *Lê 6ê a gêi a gbawoi tî?*
What is he doing with that hook?

Z: *A mǎlai la, yuu sii.*
He dances with it, you see.

Nuu kêlee a ke têi nenei nâ, fêe ê mǎla la.
Everyone who goes up into the arena must dance with it.

Z: *Kée nei ní a mãlai a ɲurîi tí da.*
But this guy is dancing with some of the wood pieces.

Ɲurîi tono tí yuu sii.
That one wood you see.

R: *Mãlai tí ve seɲ da pôkoɲ ni ee?*
That dance, isn't it imitating anything?

Z: *Mãla nô a gêi.*
It's just dance he is doing.

Nyaa ve ɓã teêi, yuu sii.
So he's not cutting the edge off you see.

Bikoo, 6a ke pai ɲule kpolui ɲa teêi veli ma i pa i too.
Because, when you are coming to cut off a ripe song from
    the drum, you come, you stand.

Ke nyaɲ ve toôi.
But then he's not standing.

R: *Kerêi e kpera nô mãla, ê kula naa?*
Didn't he just stop dancing and get out of there?

Eè-êe.   Vê too ní...di ke lôkiɲ pilii.
[No.] He didn't stand...the way when they throw *lôkiɲ*
    [dance step].

Ve tí.
It is not so.

Notes

PREFACE

[1]The films referred to here are archived at the Institut für den Wissenschaftlichen Film, Göttingen, Germany. They were studied at the Institut as preparation for the present project. Some of the films have been incorporated into the catalog of Encyclopedia Cinematografica which lends films in the United States from its facilities at Pennsylvania State University.

[2]The original Herzog and Morey cylinders are deposited at the Archives of Traditional Music, Indiana University, Bloomington, Indiana.

[3]Personal communication, Bai T. Moore, Nov. 4, 1976.

[4]Many of Okie's field recordings are deposited at the Archives of Traditional Music, Indiana University, Bloomington, Indiana.

CHAPTER 1

[1]This is not unlike the Basotho term *lipapali* analyzed by Charles R. Adams (1974).

[2]Blacking notes that ordinary experience occurs in actual time and music takes place in a world of virtual time.

CHAPTER 2

[1]This chapter, from the beginning through section
9.0, echoes and rephrases much of what has already
been stated in print by Alan P. Merriam and other
ethnomusicologists. I begin with this material to
provide background for the discussion that follows,
to tie the work here to previous study in ethnomusicology, acknowledging that these ideas have
been argued for the last decade and a half (Merriam
1964:vii-ix; 1969:213-29).

[2]See also *Musique en jeu,* a journal featuring
articles on semiotics and music, no. 1 (Nov. 1970)
- no. 28 (Sept. 1977). The terms "sound-ethnomusicologist" and "behavior-ethnomusicologist" will be
employed to describe two extreme types of ethnomusicologists. I avoid the terms "anthropologist" and
"musicologist" which do not describe with sufficient precision the individual to whom I refer.

[3]Theory here refers to the broad conceptual
framework employed by the ethnomusicologist.
Theory can also be used on a much more specific
level when referring to the explanation that ethnomusicologists derive as a result of research and
supporting data. Nettl supports this assumption
(1975:77).

[4]Though some researchers have challenged this
idea and there is some change, the assumption is
still widely held by many ethnomusicologists.

[5]For this definition I am indebted to Verlon L.
Stone. Many of his ideas are reflected in the re-
mainder of this section as well since we have
worked together in developing an interface between
theoretical orientation and media (Stone and Stone
1981).

CHAPTER 3

[1]The terms "clan" and "paramount" chiefdom apply
to boundaries drawn by the national Liberian government; they may or may not coincide with traditional
boundaries.

[2]Much of this information comes from informal discussions with Verlon L. Stone.

CHAPTER 4

[1]The evidence is based on a survey of terminology conducted in the field. See also d'Azevedo (1966:43) and Zemp (1971:72).

[2]The Woi epic is considered to contain many elements of Kpelle culture. This epic centers on the multi-episodic adventures of the superhuman hero Woi as performed by a storyteller-singer and chorus.

[3](T=text and translation of performance; numbers indicate page and line numbers for the texts). As noted in the Preface, these texts are deposited at the Archives of Traditional Music, Indiana University, Bloomington, Indiana.

[4](ATR=audio tape recording; numbers indicate tape roll and item numbers for the recordings.) As noted in the preface, these tapes are deposited at the Archives of Traditional Music.

[5]The translations in brackets indicate onomatopoeic expressions.

[6]"Light" and "heavy" are not opposites for the Kpelle. In Kpelle thinking, this is a concept and the negation of the concept rather than dialectically opposite concepts. No term exists to express the equivalent of "opposite."

[7](VTR=video tape recording.)

[8]Compare this to Ben-Amos (1975:45) and Thompson (1966:85-102).

[9]The Kpelle do not consider affect, psychomotor, and cognitive functions to be mutually exclusive categories. They divide matters according to those of the head, heart, and stomach respectively. Matters of the head would be analogous to the Western cognitive category. But matters of the heart and stomach involve both psychomotor and affective functions.

[10] The term "elusive audience" has previously been used by Dan Ben-Amos (1972:177-84).

[11] For a more detailed explanation of these terms see Alfred Schutz (1962:17-18). Compare this with the analysis of Balinese concepts in Clifford Geertz (1973:364-67).

[12] This tuning and the other tunings presented in this study have been checked with the aid of a Stroboconn.

[13] Compare this to Ben-Amos (1975:27-28).

[14] I have so far been unable to determine the meaning attributes of the tongues designated "back-of-the-song" and "neck-of-the-song."

[15] Compare this to Zemp (1971:142-44). Note that the Dan also attribute the origin of a particular drum to the chimpanzee through the human agent of a hunter.

CHAPTER 5

[1] Note the similarity of the Kpelle concept of "clearing out" for creating a performance arena to clearing out trees for creating farm areas in the forest.

[2] The choral responses in measures two and four are fixed in structure and dependent on a solo cue. Therefore, they are not relevant to the present discussion.

[3] According to the criteria, a choral entrance should also occur in measure 11 as well; the reason it does not requires further research.

[4] *Ŋâ tee* also refers to the verdict a chief offers at the conclusion of a court case.

[5] See Appendix B, Interview 1, for further explanation by an informant.

CHAPTER 6

[1]According to Liberian law, direct inquiry regarding the Poro and Sande is forbidden. Therefore
the information presented here is that which is
public knowledge and which was acquired indirectly
in the course of field research.

[2]Compare this to Lomax's correlation of melodic
structure with subsistence patterns (1968:174-90).

[3]In Kpelle society today, as these events illustrate, a few close friends and relatives gather to
mark someone's passing. In earlier times, by law
the entire village would have ceased work on the
day of the death feast, participating passively, if
not actively in the occasion.

[4]The term, Kpelle music, must be understood as
music that has long been influenced by the many
other groups living and interacting with the
Kpelle. Therefore, any Kpelle performance reflects
continued contact with various cultures over the
years of migration and settlement in the central
Kpelle area.

APPENDIX A

[1]The term *lôkiꞑ, sokokpâ,* and *kenemâ* all refer
to specific dance steps described in Chapter 4.
They will not be translated here because suitable
equivalents in English do not exist. The dance
steps are sometimes also referred to according to
the associated mnemonic drum syllables, for *lôkiꞑ*
may be called *kèleꞑ kéleꞑ* and *kenemâ* referred to
as *kpolâꞑ kpolâꞑ* or *kpâꞑ kpâꞑ.*

[2]The term *sâꞑ* is explained in Chapter 1.

[3]*Fêli* refers to the goblet drum played by the
master drummer.

References Cited

Adams, Charles R. "Ethnography of Basotho Evalua-
tive Expression in the Cognitive Domain *Lipapali*
(Games)." Ph.D. diss., Indiana University, 1974.

Adler, Guido. "Umfang, Methode, und Zeil der Musikwissenschaft." *Vierteljahrsschrift für Musikwissenschaft* 1 (1885):5-20.

Ames, David W. "Igbo and Hausa Musicians: A Comparative Examination." *Ethnomusicology* 17
(1973):250-78.

Anderson, Benjamin. *Narrative of a Journey to
Musardu, the Capitol of the Western Mandingoes*
New York: S.W. Green, 1870. London: F. Cass,
1971.

Asch, Michael. "Social Context and the Musical
Analysis of Slavey Drum Dance Songs." *Ethnomusicology* 19 (1975):245-57.

Bauman, Richard. *Verbal Art as Performance*. Rowley,
Massachusetts: Newbury House, 1977.

Becker, Howard S. "The Professional Dance Musician
and his Audience." *American Journal of Sociology*
57 (1951):136-44.

_____. *Sociological Work*. Chicago: Aldine, 1970.

_____, and Geer, Blanche. "Participant Observa-
tion and Interviewing: A Comparison." In *Symbolic interaction*, edited by Jerome G. Manis
and Bernard N. Meltzer, pp. 102-112. Boston:
Allyn and Bacon, 1972.

Bellman, Beryl L. *Village of Curers and Assassins:
On the Production of Fala Kpelle Cosmological
Categories*. The Hague: Mouton, 1975.

Ben-Amos, Dan. "The Elusive Audience of Benin Nar-
rators." *Journal of the Folklore Institute* 9
(1972):177-84.

_____. *Sweet Words: Storytelling Events in Benin*.
Philadelphia: Institute for the Study of Human
Issues, 1975.

Berger, Peter L., and Luckmann, Thomas. *The Social
Construction of Reality*. New York: Anchor, 1966.

Berreman, Gerald D. "Is Ethnoscience Relevant?" In
Culture and Cognition, edited by James P. Spradley, pp. 223-32. San Francisco: Chandler, 1972.

Besmer, Fremont E. "An Hausa Song from Katsina."
Ethnomusicology 14 (1970):418-38.

_____. *Kídàn dárán sállà: Music for the Eve of the
Muslim Festivals of 'Id Al-Fatir and 'Id Al-Kabir
in Kano, Nigeria*. Bloomington: African Studies
Program, Indiana University, 1974.

Birdwhistell, Ray L. *Kinesics and Context*. Philadelphia: University of Pennsylvania Press, 1970.

Blacking, John. *Venda Children's Songs*. Johannes-
burg: Witwatersrand University Press, 1967.

_____. "Deep and Surface Structures in Venda
Music." *Yearbook of the International Folk Music
Council* 3 (1971a):91-108.

_____. "Toward a Theory of Musical Competence."
In *Man: Anthropological Essays Presented to O.F.
Raum,* pp. 19-34. Capetown: Struik, 1971b.

_____. "Field Work in African Music." In *Reflec-
tions on Afro-American Music,* edited by Domi-
nique-Rene DeLerma, pp. 207-21. Kent: Kent State
University Press, 1973.

_____. *How Musical is Man?* Seattle: University of
Washington Press, 1973.

Blumer, Herbert. *Symbolic Interactionism: Perspec-*
tive and Method. Englewood Cliffs: Prentice-
Hall, 1969.

Boilès, Charles. "Tepehua Thought-Song: A Case of
Semantic Signaling." *Ethnomusicology* 11 (1967):
267-92.

_____, and Nattiez, Jean-Jacques. "Petite his-
toire critique de l'ethnomusicologie." *Musique*
en jeu, no. 28 (1977):26-53.

Boon, James. "Further Operations of 'Culture' in
Anthropology: A Synthesis of and for Debate."
In *The Idea of Culture in the Social Sciences,*
edited by Louis Schneider and Charles Bonjean,
pp. 1-32. Cambridge: Cambridge University Press,
1973.

Brown, Richard H. "The Emergence of Existential
Thought: Philosophical Perspectives on Posi-
tivist and Humanist Forms of Social Theory."
In *Existential Sociology,* edited by Jack D.
Douglas and John M. Johnson, pp. 77-100. Cam-
bridge: Cambridge University Press, 1977a.

_____. *A Poetic for Sociology*. Cambridge: Cam-
bridge University Press, 1977b.

Büttikofer, Johann. *Reisebilder aus Liberia*. 2 vols.
Leiden: E.J. Brill, 1890.

Casthelain, J. *La Langue guerzé; Grammaire, diction-*
naire. Mémoires, no. 20. Dakar: Institut Fonda-
mental d'Afrique Noire, 1952.

Cicourel, Aaron V. *Method and Measurement in Soci-*
ology. New York: Free Press, 1964.

_____. *Cognitive Sociology: Language and Meaning*
in Social Interaction. Harmondsworth: Penguin
Education, 1973.

Cole, Michael [and others]. *The Cultural Context of*
Learning and Thinking. New York: Basic Books,
1971.

d'Azevedo, Warren L. "Some Historical Problems in
the Delineation of a Central West Atlantic

Region." *Annals of the New York Academy of Sciences* 96 (1962):512-38.

_____. *The Artist Archetype in Gola Culture*. Preprint no. 14. Desert Research Institute: University of Nevada, 1966.

Delafosse, Maurice. "Un État Nègre: La République de Liberia." *Bulletin du Comité de l'Afrique Française, Renseignments Coloniaux* 9 (1900).

Ekman, Paul, and Friesen, Wallace. "A Tool for the Analysis of Motion Picture Film or Videotape." *American Psychologist* 24 (1969):240-43.

Feld, Steven. "Linguistic Models in Ethnomusicology." *Ethnomusicology* 18 (1974):197-217.

Fulton, Richard. "The Kpelle of Liberia: A Study of Political Change in the Liberian Interior." Ph.D. diss., University of Connecticut, 1969.

Gay, John H., and Cole, Michael. *The New Mathematics and an Old Culture; A Study of Learning Among the Kpelle of Liberia*. New York: Holt, Rinehart, and Winston, 1967.

Geertz, Clifford. *The Interpretation of Cultures*. New York: Basic Books, 1973.

Germain, J. "L'Au-delà Chez les Guerzé." *Études Guinéenes* 2 (1947):27-35.

_____. "Extrait d'une monographie des habitants du cercle de N'zérékoré." *Études Guinéenes* 13 (1955):3-54.

Germann, Paul. *Die Völkerstamme im Norden von Liberia*. Leipzig: R. Voigtländer, 1933.

Gibbs, James L. "The Judicial Implication of Marital Instability Among the Kpelle." Ph.D. diss., Harvard University, 1960.

_____. "The Kpelle of Liberia." In *People of Africa*, pp. 197-240. New York: Holt, Rinehart, and Winston, 1965.

Goffman, Erving. *The Presentation of Self in Every-*
day Life. New York: Doubleday, 1959.

Gourlay, Kenneth A. "Towards a Reassessment of the
Ethnomusicologist's Role in Research." *Ethno-*
musicology 22 (1978):1-35.

Greenberg, Joseph. *The Languages of Africa*. Bloomington: Indiana University, 1966.

Hair, P.E.H. "An Account of the Liberian Hinterland
c. 1780." *Sierra Leone Studies* 16 (1962):218-26.

Hansen, Judith Friedman. "Symbolic Interactionist
Approaches to Social Organization and Culture."
Unpublished MS, 1974.

Harley, George W. *Masks as Agents of Social Control*
in Northeast Liberia. Papers of the Peabody
Museum, vol. 32, no. 2. Cambridge: Harvard University, 1950.

Herndon, Marcia. "The Cherokee Ballgame Cycle: An
Ethnomusicologist's View." *Ethnomusicology* 15
(1971):340.

Herzog, George. "Speech-Melody and Primitive Music."
Musical Quarterly 20 (1934):452-66.

_____. "Drum-Signalling in a West African Tribe."
Word 1 (1945):217-38.

_____. "Canon in West African Xylophone Melodies."
Journal of the American Musicological Society 2
(1949):196-97.

Himmelheber, Hans G., and Ulrike. *Die Dan, Ein*
Bauernvolk im Westafrikanischen Urwald. Stutt-
gart: W. Kohlhammer, 1958.

Holas, B. "Décès d'une femme guerzé." *Africa* 23
(1953):145-55.

Hood, Mantle. "Ethnomusicology." *Harvard Dictionary*
of Music, 1969 ed., pp. 298-300.

_____. *The Ethnomusicologist*. New York: McGraw
Hill, 1971.

Husserl, Edmund. *The Phenomenology of Internal Time-Consciousness*. Bloomington: Indiana University Press, 1964.

Hymes, Dell. "Introduction: Toward Ethnographies of Communication." *American Anthropologist* 66, no. 6 (1964):1-34.

Johnston, Sir Harry. *Liberia*. 2 vols. London: Hutchinson, 1906.

Kaeppler, Adrienne L. "Structure of Tongan Dance." *Ethnomusicology* 16 (1972):173-217.

Knowlton, James Q. *A Socio- and Psycho-linguistic Theory of Pictorial Communication*. Bloomington: Indiana University, Division of Instructional Systems Technology, 1964.

Lassort, Rev. P. "La Langue kpèlè." *Études Guinéenes* 2 (1947):21-25.

_____. "L'Écriture guerzé." *Première Conférence Internationale de Africanistes de l'Ouest* 1945, Comptes rendus, 2 (1951):209-15.

Liberia, Government of Liberia. *Summary Report, Population Census of Liberia*. 1962

Liberia, Government of Liberia. *Economic Survey of Liberia*. 1968.

Liberia, Ministry of Planning and Economic Affairs. *1974 Census of Population and Housing, Population Bulletin, no. 2*, 1976.

List, George. "The Boundaries of Speech and Song." *Ethnomusicology* 7 (1963):1-16.

Lomax, Alan. *Folk Song Style and Culture*. Washington: American Association for the Advancement of Science, 1968.

McAllester, David P. *Enemy Way Music*. Papers of the Peabody Museum, vol. 41, no. 3. Cambridge: Harvard University, 1954.

_____, and McCollester, Roxanne, eds. "Whither Ethnomusicology?"*Ethnomusicology* 3 (1959):99-105.

McLeod, Norma. "Some Techniques of Analysis for
    non-Western Music." Ph.D. diss., Northwestern
    University, 1966.

Mengrelis, Thanos. "L'Initiation chez les Guerzés."
    Notes Africaines 29 (1946):22-25.

_____. "La Voix des *niamou* chez les Guerzé de la
    Guinee française." *Notes Africaines* 38 (1948):8.

_____. "La Sortie des inities en pays Guerzé."
    Notes Africaines 50 (1951):44-46.

_____. "Le Sens des masques dan l'initiation chez
    les Guerzé de la Guinee française." *Africa* 22
    (1952):257-62.

Merriam, Alan P. *The Anthropology of Music.* Evan-
    ston: Northwestern University Press, 1964.

_____. "Ethnomusicology Revisited." *Ethnomusi-
    cology* 13 (1969):213-29.

_____. "Ethnomusicology Today." *Current Musi-
    cology,* no. 20 (1975):50-66.

_____. "Analysis of African Musical Rhythm and
    Concepts of Time-Reckoning." Paper presented at
    the Society for Ethnomusicology Annual Meeting.
    Austin, Texas, November 4, 1977.

Midgett, Douglas K. "Performance Roles and Musical
    Change in a Carribean Society." *Ethnomusicology*
    21 (1977):55-73.

Moore, Bai T. "Categories of Traditional Liberian
    Songs." *Liberian Studies Journal* 2 (1970):117-
    37.

Murphy, William P. "A Semantic and Logical Analysis
    of Kpelle Proverb Metaphors of Secrecy." Ph.D.
    diss., Stanford University, 1976.

Nattiez, Jean-Jacques. "A Contribution of Musical
    Semiotics to the Semiotic Discussion in General."
    In *A Perfusion of Signs,* edited by Thomas A.
    Sebeok, pp. 134-36.

Nauta, Doede. *The Meaning of Information*. Paris: Mouton, 1972.

Nettl, Bruno. *Theory and Method in Ethnomusicology*. New York: Free Press, 1964.

_____. "The State of Research in Ethnomusicology and Recent Developments." *Current Musicology*, no. 20 (1975):67-78.

Oxford English Dictionary. 2 vols. Oxford: Clarion Press, 1971.

Phillips, Derek L. *Knowledge From What?* Chicago: Rand McNally, 1971.

Phillipson, Michael. "Theory, Methodology and Conceptualization," and "Phenomenological Philosophy and Sociology." In *New Directions in Sociological Theory*, pp. 77-116, 119-63. Cambridge: MIT Press, 1972.

Picot, J. "N'zérékoré," *Annales Africaines, Monographies d'Afrique Noire*. Paris: Guillemot et Lamonthe, 1958, pp. 273-86.

Polyani, Michael. *The Tacit Dimension*. Garden City, New York: Anchor, 1966.

Robertson-DeCarbo, Carol. "Tayil: Musical Communication and Social Organization Among the Mapuche of Argentina." Ph.D. diss., Indiana University, 1975.

Royce, Anya Peterson. *The Anthropology of Dance*. Bloomington: Indiana University Press, 1977.

Sachs, Nahoma. "Music and Meaning: Musical Symbolism in a Macedonian Village." Ph.D. diss., Indiana University, 1975.

Schaeffner, André. *Les Kissi: Une Société noire et ses instruments de musique*. Paris: Hermann et Cie, 1951.

Schutz, Alfred. *Collected Papers I: The Problem of Social Reality*. The Hague: Martinus Nijhoff, 1962.

_____. *Collected Papers II: Studies in Social Theory*. The Hague: Martinus Nijhoff, 1964.

_____, and Luckmann, Thomas. *The Structures of the Life World*. Evanston: Northwestern University Press, 1973.

Schwab, George. *Tribes of the Liberian Hinterland*. Peabody Museum Papers, vol. 31. Cambridge: Harvard University, 1947.

Seeger, Charles. "Factorial Analysis of the Song as an Approach to the formation of a Unitary Field Theory for Musicology." *Journal of the International Folk Music Council* 20 (1966):33-39.

_____. "Reflection upon a Given Topic: Music in Universal Perspective." *Ethnomusicology* 15, (1971):385-98.

Spradley, James P. *You Owe Yourself a Drunk*. Boston: Little, Brown, 1970.

Stone, Verlon L., and Stone, Ruth M. "Event, Feedback and Analysis: Research Media in the Study of Music Events." *Ethnomusicology* 25 (1981): 215-25.

Strong, Richard P., ed. *The African Republic of Liberia and the Belgian Congo*. vol. 1. Cambridge: Harvard University Press, 1930.

Sturtevant, William C. "Studies in Ethnoscience." In *Culture and Cognition*, edited by James P. Spradley, pp. 120-67. San Francisco: Chandler, 1972.

Thompson, Robert Farris. "An Aesthetic of the Cool: West African Dance." *African Forum* 2 (1966):85-102.

von Ballmoos, Agnes Nebo. "Liberian Music." *Liberian Research Association Journal* 3 (1970):30-39.

Welmers, William. *Basic Dictionary of Spoken Kpelle*. Monrovia, Liberia: Lutheran Mission, 1948.

_____. "Secret Medicines, Magic, and Rites of the Kpelle Tribe in Liberia." *Southwestern Journal of Anthropology* 5 (1949):208-43.

_____, and Spehr, Otto. *Spoken Kpelle*. 1st rev. ed. Monrovia, Liberia: Lutheran Church in Liberia, 1956.

Westermann, Diedrich. *Die Kpelle: Ein Negerstamm in Liberia*. Göttingen: Vandenhoeck and Ruprecht, 1921.

_____. *Die Kpelle-Sprache in Liberia: Grammatische Einführung, Texte, und Wörterbuch*. Berlin: D. Reimer, 1924.

Whitehurst, D.W. "Whitehurst Journal." *African Repository* 12 (1836):105-315.

Worth, Sol. "The Development of a Semiotic of Film." *Semiotica* 1 (1969):282-321.

Zemp, Hugo. "Aspects of 'Are'Are Musical Theory." *Ethnomusicology* 23 (1979):5-48.

_____, *Musique dan*. Paris: Mouton, 1971.

Recordings Cited

Alberts, Arthur S., coll. *Tribal, Folk and Cafe Music of West Africa*. Field Recordings, twelve 78 rpm discs in 3 vol., 1950. Reissued as *The Field Recordings of African Coast Rhythms: Tribal and Folk Music of West Africa, Recorded in French Guinea, Gold Coast, Ivory Coast, Upper Volta, and Liberia*. Riverside RLP-4001, one 12" LP disc, 1953; and *The Field Recordings of New Songs in the African Coast*. Riverside RLP-4003, one 12" LP disc, 1954.

Okie, Packard L., coll. *Folk Music of Liberia*. Folkways, FE 4465, 1955, 1960.

Sarkesian, Leo. coll. *Music Time in Liberia*. Tempo International, TLM 67, c. 1966-70.

Stone, Ruth M., and Stone, Verlon L., coll. *Music of the Kpelle of Liberia*. Folkways, FE 4385, 1972.

Index

174